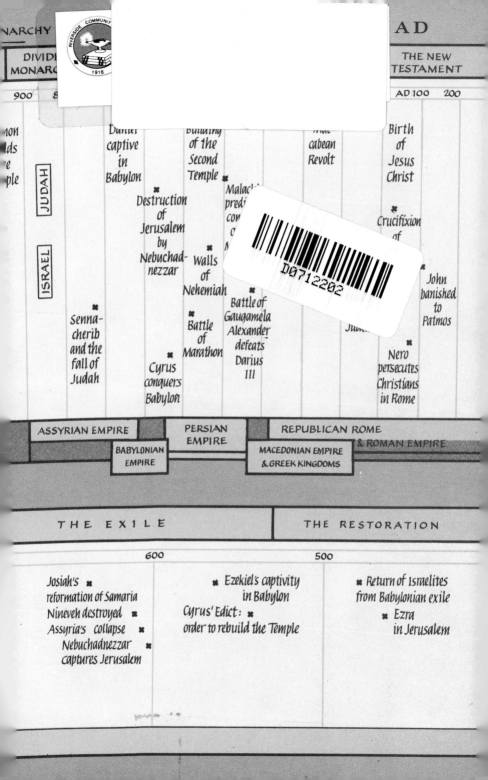

900 8   AD 100   200

JUDAH

ISRAEL

Daniel captive in Babylon

Building of the Second Temple

cabean Revolt

Birth of Jesus Christ

✳ Destruction of Jerusalem by Nebuchad-nezzar

Malac predi con o M

✳ Crucifixion of

✳ Walls of Nehemiah

✳ Battle of Gaugamela Alexander defeats Darius III

✳ Senna-cherib and the fall of Judah

✳ Battle of Marathon

✳ Cyrus conquers Babylon

John banished to Patmos

Juda

✳ Nero persecutes Christians in Rome

| ASSYRIAN EMPIRE | PERSIAN EMPIRE | REPUBLICAN ROME | |
| BABYLONIAN EMPIRE | | MACEDONIAN EMPIRE & GREEK KINGDOMS | & ROMAN EMPIRE |

THE EXILE | THE RESTORATION

600   500

Josiah's ✳ reformation of Samaria
Nineveh destroyed ✳
Assyria's collapse ✳
Nebuchadnezzar ✳ captures Jerusalem

✳ Ezekiel's captivity in Babylon
Cyrus' Edict: ✳ order to rebuild the Temple

✳ Return of Israelites from Babylonian exile
✳ Ezra in Jerusalem

THE
ROOTS OF JESUS

PALESTINE
OF THE
NEW TESTAMENT

MT. HERMON

Caesarea
Philippi

TRACHONITIS

LAKE
SEMECHONITIS

Tyre

SYRO-PHOENICIA

Ptolemais
(Acco, Akka)

Chorazin
Capernaum
Gennesaret
Cana (?)   Magdala
GALILEE
Cana (?)
Nazareth
MT. TABOR
Naim

Bethsaida Julias
SEA OF GALILEE
Gergesa

Tiberias

R. YARMUK

Gadara

MT. CARMEL

DECAPOLIS

Caesarea

Scythopolis

Pella

SAMARIA

Aenon

Sebaste
(Samaria)

MT. EBAL
MT. GERIZIM
Sychar

Caesaria
Stratonis

RIVER JORDAN

R. JABBOK

PERAEA

Antipatris

Joppa
(Jaffa)

Arimathaea

Ephraim

Philadelphia

Lydda

Jericho

Emmaus(?)

Jerusalem Qumran
Ain Karim
Bethany
Bethlehem

Bethany
Beyond
Jordan

MEDITERRANEAN SEA

Ascalon

JUDAEA

Machaerus

Gaza

Hebron

R. ARNON

DEAD
SEA

IDUMAEA

R. ZERED

0   MILES   30
0   KM   30

THE
ROOTS OF JESUS

A Genealogical Investigation

JAMES B. BELL

EDITED BY RICHARD I. ABRAMS

1983
Doubleday & Company, Inc.
Garden City, New York

Riverside Community College
Library
4800 Magnolia Avenue
Riverside, California 92506

Biblical quotations are from the King James Version of the Bible.

Library of Congress Cataloging in Publication Data

Bell, James B.
   The Roots of Jesus.

   Bibliography.
   Includes index.
   1. Jesus Christ—Genealogy. I. Title.
BT314.B39 1983   232.9'01 [B]
ISBN 0-385-18062-4
Library of Congress Catalog Card Number: 81-43738

COPYRIGHT © 1983 BY JAMES B. BELL
ALL RIGHTS RESERVED
PRINTED IN THE UNITED STATES OF AMERICA
FIRST EDITION

CONTENTS

LIST OF ILLUSTRATIONS

PREFACE

Today there is much interest in family history triggered in no small way by Alex Haley's engaging and moving book *Roots*. Its adaptation as a widely watched television series introduced many people from every ethnic and economic background to the delight in knowing about their family's past. For after all, the family, in both the Eastern and Western world, is the oldest social institution, older in form than any monarchy or any religion. It is in the family that we have been born and trained to take our place in society. It is from the family that we go out to establish the cycle all over again with our own children. It is within the family group that we learn our religious and moral precepts and have our minds awakened to educational and cultural knowledge.

The purpose of this book is to consider the roots of Jesus. As the greatest man who has ever lived, we want to know more about him, about his life and ministry, about his preaching, teaching and healing, and about his family. Our resources are the accounts of Jesus' family's genealogy in the Bible, particularly the Gospels of Matthew and Luke. However, these biblical accounts, much as Alex Haley discovered about his family when he visited his ancestral village in West Africa, are based on oral traditions. They are not supported by the wealth of public documents with which you and I are familiar as we compile and write our own family's story. We cannot hold in our hands a certified photocopy of Jesus' birth certificate or a copy of his parents' marriage license. We cannot write to an archives center or public records office, either of the state or a church, and ask for an official copy of the record of Jesus' baptism in the Jordan River. According to modern day standards of historical research, we are unable to document Jesus' genealogy, but we are able to discuss the rich biblical traditions regarding his roots.

Why study Jesus' "roots"? We believe that this question mirrors something about ourselves and the world we have inherited.

We live in a world of renewed interest in the life and teachings of Jesus. The Evangelical Movement . . . a countermovement to this age of science and nuclear weaponry . . . has stirred the hearts and minds of people everywhere. It is an age when the anxiety-ridden peoples of this world are searching for moral and spiritual roots to serve as an anchor in this time of accelerating and ever-changing social, political and economic conditions.

Jesus through his life and teachings represents an inspired and inspiring model for individual behavior. Because of his life example, we want to know more about his life, about his humanity and about his divinity. We want to know the roots of Jesus to the extent that they can shed light on all our roots . . . our common heritage and perhaps our common destiny. The influence of Jesus on the course of Western civilization during the past two thousand years is apparent everywhere: Our ears are at once engaged by the sounds and strains of ancient or modern hymns which describe in words and music the Messiah's story and message; our eyes are focused on the architectural styles and buildings inspired by the Christian message through the ages in Jerusalem, Rome and Canterbury as well as in every city, town and hamlet of our country.

This book is designed to be of interest to a general audience of readers and not merely to a small coterie of theologians and scholars. It is to be a popular study of Jesus' roots, his genealogy, and as such, we hope it can kindle the spark of insight and self-renewal so essential to all of us in meeting the challenges of this age of uncertainty and promise.

The structure of this book is straightforward and simple, yet a brief word of guidance may be useful. The first chapter considers the use of genealogy in the myths and royal families of the powerful civilizations which surrounded and touched the Jews, particularly the Egyptians, Babylonians and Greeks. The four following chapters explore in turn the genealogies of Jesus as noted in Matthew and Luke, and Mark and John's understanding of who Jesus was. We next look at the significance of the genealogy of the House of David not only in the Old Testament writings but also in the social and political history of the Jews; and the writings of historians and theologians through the past two thousand years on the topic of Jesus' roots. There are three genealogical charts, to guide us in our discussion of Jesus' genealogy: a chart each for the ancestors noted in the Gospels of Matthew and Luke and one for the House of David. Throughout the book I have used the King James version of the Bible for all scripture citations.

First and foremost, I would like to extend special thanks to my friend and collaborator, Richard I. Abrams, who initially conceived of the idea of a book on *The Roots of Jesus*. It was Dick who recognized the rather unique convergence in my own background—as a graduate of a theological school, a professional historian and author of the reference book *Searching for Your Ancestors*—as being well-suited to the authorship of such a work. For his help also in shaping and editing the overall manuscript and in placing the manuscript with our publisher, Doubleday, I am most grateful.

I am particularly indebted to Leslie Choquette, who attentively understood my research needs as the project was launched, and at every step along the way provided me with aid and guidance. I am also indebted to the editor of the *Harvard Theological Review*, Gary A. Bisbee, who provided me with much information and important critical direction for Chapter VII with details relating to the history of the messianic idea among the Jews as well as the discussions among early church historians and theologians regarding Jesus' roots.

The publishers have been unfailingly kind, supportive and congenial. All the faults and errors of fact or judgment in the book (and I have no doubt there are a few) are of my own making.

James B. Bell
Director
The New-York Historical Society
New York City

THE
ROOTS OF JESUS

I

THE HISTORICAL SETTING: MYTHS AND GENEALOGIES

The concern with family history is an age-old interest. Since the dawn of civilization in the Fertile Crescent bounded by the Tigris and Euphrates rivers in the Near East, humanity has been concerned with the roots of their families and their gods. Long before the writing of history on the walls of caves, on clay tablets or on rolls of papyrus, a family's genealogy was remembered orally by a member of the family or tribe who passed along the genealogical account from one generation to the next. We all recall one relative or another in our family today who seems to know not only the broad outlines of the family's past but also many of the details. Ever ready to spin their knowledge to those who will listen, they are perhaps a bit reticent about putting pen to paper and recording in permanent fashion the family's genealogy.

The word genealogy is an old one, derived from two Greek terms—*genos*, which means race, and *logos*, which means discourse or an orderly form of speaking or writing. Simply, it is the study of the origins, descent and relationships of families. Throughout the Middle East, in the ancient worlds of Egypt, Babylonia, Phoenicia, the Greek city-states, Rome and among the early Hebrews and the Jews of the day of Jesus there is one common continuing strand of interest, an attachment to genealogy in the religious and political life of the community, as well as in the intimacy of the family.

The myths of the antique world, traditional stories about gods, kings and heroes, became the model for royal and priestly genealogies in every nation. Myths would often describe the manner in which the world was created and how gods created humans. They frequently describe relationships between several gods and between gods and mortals. Myths were also used to remind the listeners of the lives of heroes who represented the highest ideals of a society. They deal too with the large, complex and important aspects of human and superhuman existence.

We may be diverted in reading about the many incredible, comic, barbaric, monstrous or romantic occurrences in many myths. Nonetheless, generally the accounts have a certain distinction and eloquence because they do address timely and timeless matters of human interest.

Egypt. Egyptian religion, which lasted for 3,500 years, had ancient unchronicled origins. The Egyptians saw divinity in everything and everywhere: in the sun, moon and stars; in animals and kings; in birth and death; in river, desert and vegetation. They created an enormous and confusing legion of gods.

The Egyptians, unlike the Greeks, did not make their gods in their image. Ancient Egyptian myths described gods in animal shapes, and the name of each god was spelled in hieroglyphs beside the beast or bird. Thus, the jackal stands for Anubis, the hawk for Horus and the frog for Heqet. The animals were the object of strictly local worship, as different cities had their different beast-gods: Apis, the bull, was the god of Memphis; Ba, the goat, of Mendes; Bast, the cat, of Bubastis.

Though Egypt was rich in gods, such as Osiris, Isis and Horus, her literature is not abundant in myths. The religious books which have survived are, as a rule, hymns, litanies and the funeral service, the "Book of the Dead." In these works the myths are taken for granted and not told in full.

For the ancient Egyptians only the king and the gods played a role in mythology. The king was the only mediator and tie between humanity and the gods. The king of Egypt was looked upon in the First Dynasty, about 3000 B.C., as the god Horus, who was embodied in the image of a seated or standing falcon. Accordingly, Horus was acknowledged as the ruler of all Egypt, heavenly king and the falcon. It was through Horus that the Egyptians identified and linked the mythological genealogy to the nine gods who gave birth to the universe—to Egypt, to heaven and earth. It is through Horus and his father, Osiris, and his father, Geb, and his father, Shu, and his father, Atum, that the Egyptian kings established their mythological genealogy as well as their identification. Thus, a genealogy of five generations was established to prove the divine and primeval character of the king.

Genealogies were not common later among the Egyptians of the Old Kingdom (2800–2250 B.C.). For the next thousand years it is nearly always the individual, the aristocrat or royal personage, not the family, who is the focus of attention. A genealogy of seven generations, noted at the beginning of the eighteenth dynasty (c. 1580 B.C.), and another reaching back to the grandfather in the following dynasty provide the exceptions. Complete genealogical trees appear only in subsequent eras of Egyptian history tied to the Ethiopian kings (712–663 B.C.), the Psammetichi (663–609 B.C.), and the Persians (525–404 B.C.).

The monuments which punctuate the shoreline of the Valley of the Nile illustrate that the upper-class and royal families of ancient Egypt took interest and pride in their family's genealogy. The world's first systematic genealogist was an Egyptian nobleman, Prince Khnumhotep II, who recorded on the walls of his tomb at Beni Hassan: "I have kept alive the names of my fathers, which I found obliterated upon the doorways [making them] legible in form, accurate in reading, not putting one in the place of another."

Babylonia. The Babylonians produced a literary masterpiece in the *Epic of Gilgamesh.* Most records of Babylonian myths date from about 700 B.C., when they were transcribed in cuneiform on clay tablets and placed in the library of the Assyrian King Ashurbanipol at Nineveh. However, the Gilgamesh epic is at least 1,500 years older than Homer, originating about 2000 B.C. Gilgamesh, the hero of the legend, is the wise, powerful but tyrannical king of the ancient Sumerian city of Uruk. He was two-thirds a god and one-third a mortal, famed for his adventures in war, for his cleverness as an unbeatable wrestler and for his constant lustfulness. The story records the episodes of the King of Uruk in his fruitless search for immortality and of his friendship with Enkider, the wild man from the hills. It is also of more than passing interest for our attention as included in the epic is another legend of the Flood which agrees in many details with the biblical story of Noah.

Greece. Greek mythology has been an inspiration of Western art and literature for more than two thousand years. It forms the richest and most fertile collection of stories in Western civilization since most of the world mythology is Greek mythology, read to children and taught in school. The myths produced an abundance of heroes: adventurers who tended to be fighters—bold, experienced, fierce, strong and frequently clever. Their accomplishments were several steps above those of mere mortals. However, they also had serious shortcomings that sometimes brought them to ruin: flaws such as unhesitating pride, impulsiveness, cruelty—which arose from the very source of their successes—ambition. With Greek heroes, ambition was forceful and dynamic, occasionally aspiring to godlike powers. They were models of human excellence providing standards for Greek youths to follow.

The myths of tragic dynasties show this same ambivalence. Despite their worldly power, the royal families of Crete, Mycenae, Thebes and Athens were scarred with their own particular weaknesses that marked them vulnerable to disaster: pride of power, ruthlessness in getting revenge, stubbornness in pursuing some goal and sexual conflict. No race has understood as clearly as the Greeks that character is destiny and heroic and tragic elements occasionally proceed from the same seed.

The age of Greek supremacy in the Mediterranean world lasted from about 450–325 B.C. It was during this period that the people of the Greek peninsula built a thriving network of city-states and trading colonies as far east as the shores of the Black Sea, and along the coast of North Africa, to Sicily and southern Italy and to Marseilles. It has been said that the history of nations and of people grew out of mythology. The religions of ancient Greece and Rome were based on such mythology. While the divinities of Mount Olympus do not have a single worshipper among living men and women today, their interest in genealogy shaped not only the manner of worship of their gods, but also the story of the origins and development of ancient Greece.

Throughout history, the religion of each cultural or social group, such as the Greeks, Egyptians, Romans and Hebrews, included an explanation of how the world was created, how people came into being and exactly what their relationship to their creator was. The human race, in return for this gift of life, owed respect to its creating spirits or gods, and each society developed rituals of worship in order to ensure the creator's goodwill. The influence of these gods was great: Everyday existence and the laws of the society were governed by them. By worshiping and offering appropriate gifts, humans believed good fortune would follow. Also, if misfortune or disaster occurred, it was a sign that humans had insulted the gods or were in some way out of favor and out of step with them.

The pages of Homer's heroic poems, *The Iliad* and *The Odyssey*, recount the exploits of Greek gods and heroes: gods such as Zeus, Poseidon and Hades and heroes like Heracles, Jason and Odysseus. In every case the legends of ancient Greece included a genealogy which traced the hero's or god's ancestry to an earlier ancestor who was either a god or semidivine human being. The continuous pedigrees of gods and heroes tied present men with a common source of existence. The tie was an unbroken line of descent between the gods and the heroes. The genealogies included accounts which were at once human and historical as well as divine and mythological.

There are several important characteristics of Greek genealogies. First, every democracy, race, religious group or political body had its own genealogy. Second, the first genealogies used drew upon local names familiar to the people such as rivers, lakes, mountains, valleys and villages embodied as persons. Furthermore, they were often called either kings or chiefs. Third, the genealogies included women as well as men; legends of women or heroines were of importance as were the wives and daughters of Greek heroes. Fourth, for a public without written records, the oral traditions of each generation were preserved and passed on to succeeding generations as genealogies, stories and religious narratives. Only much later were these accounts written down.

Finally, irregularities and discrepancies in genealogies while frequent seem to have been neither surprising nor offensive to either the teller or the listener. The value of genealogies was not in their length but in their continuity over the centuries; not in the power of setting out a prolonged list of human parents and grandparents, but in the sense of a relationship with a primitive ancestor. It is a blending of the past with the present: a blending of gods and mortals. Never before or since have gods been so much like humans except, of course, in their ability to die.

Israel and the Old Testament. We do not know when the tradition of recording genealogies became established in Israel, although we do know it is an ancient one. Lists of families and of citizens for official civil purposes must have been made very early, as suggested by the Census of David noted in II Samuel 24:2. At several other points in the Bible it is apparent the Israelites were familiar with such an enumeration. At the time of the giving of the Deuteronomic law there must have been some set procedure for determining whether a person was of pure Israeli descent. Like other Semitic peoples in the Near East, the Israelites traced the ancestry of their tribe, clan or individual back through the male line to a historical or mythical figure of the dim past. It was from that figure that they took their name. For example, the individuals of a group of people would be known as the sons of Israel while the group would be known as the house of Israel. Membership in the tribe or clan meant that the individual was descended naturally or by adoption from a common ancestry. The member of a tribe or clan was then able to point to Jacob, the father of all the tribes, as his great ancestor. Accordingly, the important role of genealogy in ancient Israel illustrates a society strongly based on a tribal and patriarchal tradition.

The genealogies in the Old Testament seem to have been written during the period between the sixth and fourth century B.C., following the Exile of the Hebrews in Egypt and at about the time of the Persian conquest of Israel. We find genealogies in several books of the Old Testament: Genesis, Exodus, Leviticus, Numbers, Deuteronomy, I and II Chronicles, Ezra and Nehemiah. Some have parallels in Babylonian writings, such as Genesis chapters 4 and 5 which recount the birth of Cain and Abel, the murder of Abel and the genealogy of Adam's son Seth; terminating with the note that Noah lived for five hundred years and was the father of Shem, Ham and Japheth. Other genealogies, such as those recorded in Genesis chapters 10 and 11, serve a different purpose: They recount a history of God's chosen people. The genealogies describe the important epochs in Israel's history and the events and persons through whom God acted: from creation to Exile in Egypt to the building of the Temple. As the story unwinds in Genesis chapters 10 and 11, the genealogy of Noah's family, his sons and his sons' sons, illustrates that it was no accident that God chose Israel as his people and that a special and unique relationship was thereby fashioned.

Furthermore, the account is a chronology of nations, presenting the geographical and political relationships in the form of a genealogy or family tree branching out from the three sons of Noah. In the ancient world this manner of epochal genealogy, from one major historical event to another, was well understood. Genesis, Chapter 2 gives the names of certain outstanding personages in their correct genealogical line, but not always in a father-to-son sequence. Consequently, the length of time covered is much longer than it appears. For example, we do not know the precise date of the Flood which covered the earth. Without that information we have difficulty identifying the date of Adam and Eve. The only way we can possibly set an approximate date of the Flood is to follow the family line of Adam to the time of the Flood, using the genealogies and chronologies as recorded in Genesis, chapters 5 and 7, verses 11–24.

After the Exile in Egypt, genealogies became so important that significant figures, such as Samuel (I Samuel, Chapter 1), the last of the judges and the first of the prophets after Moses who anointed Saul and later David as king, who previously had no recorded genealogy, was provided with a family tree. To preserve the ancient historical identity as well as the continuing links of the nation and of its faith, it was considered essential to maintain given lines of ancestors for the nation's political and religious leaders. Genealogical lists detailed individual family history, particularly those of families who played important historical roles, such as the house of David, the house of Saul and the house of Zadok. For Israel, it was important to maintain genealogies to indicate the people's distinctive relationship with God and to prevent the dilution of their religious beliefs and practices. One solution was to require that the priests and political leaders be of pure Jewish blood (Nehemiah 7:5–67).

No one was permitted to become priest and enter the service of the Temple unless he could present a perfect and authentic genealogical record of his priestly descent. During the period of the Second Temple, about 510 B.C., purity of descent played a vital role, especially for the priests and those Israelite families whose daughters were eligible to marry priests. The priests, in order to preserve their pure status, were restricted to marriage ties with families of unquestioned purity of descent. They were therefore required to know in detail their own genealogy and that of the families whose daughters they married. Families laying claim to purity of blood kept ancestral lists, which served as evidence of their seniority and legitimacy. Possession of such lists further strengthened their family's standing in the community. A master genealogical list was kept in the Temple, noting genealogical details on all priestly families. Such a master list was maintained and verified by a special priestly council. Furthermore, it was the custom that even the offices of the Temple service passed from father to son, from generation to generation.

Thus, the priests were exceedingly careful in preserving the documents that gave the necessary qualifications to their sacred office. With these records they kept the Book of the Law (the Pentateuch, the first five books of the Bible) which, as we have noted, described in epochal fashion all of the early part of Jewish history. Aside from the priestly class, ordinary genealogies were based on oral tradition.

Following the destruction of the Temple in 587 B.C., whereby the priestly class lost its physical center, the priests placed even more emphasis and value on the purity of their genealogical roots to ensure their continuing social prominence.

After the return from Exile in Babylon to Zion, other privileged groups besides the priests were interested in establishing and maintaining their social and economic position through genealogy. Such genealogies were essential to reclaim and preserve ancient family properties. These efforts were supported by the ancient genealogical lists referred to in the opening chapters of Chronicles including the genealogies of the Patriarchs and the Twelve Sons of Israel. Once again the theme is clearly one of intertwining individual and family history.

The ancient compilers and editors of the genealogical lists in the Bible, especially those of I Chronicles, were faced with addressing conflicting lists and traditions, often mutually contradictory. The union of various lists, without changing their distinctiveness, was possible because the editors of these extensive lists regarded them as genealogies of individuals, the forebears of families and tribes. For them the repeated recurrence of the same name provided no trouble: They did not regard such repetition as conflicting detail but simply as showing that the same name kept reappearing among individuals related to one another.

Purity of blood played an important role in the political designs of prominent tribal families for secular power, and even the royal houses had to resort to genealogical proofs in order to strengthen their position. Accordingly, the Hasmoneans, who had to protect themselves against the contention that only descendants of David could lay claim to kingship, challenged the purity of David's blood because of his descent from Ruth the Moabite. Herod, who also had to face attack as to the legitimacy of his rule, fashioned for himself a pedigree back to David, after first destroying relevant genealogical records maintained in the Temple.

Where pedigrees of generations from antiquity are given in the Bible, such as Genesis 5, 11:10–26, I Chronicles 2:9–12, 6:1–48, they probably do not rest on authentic records but are assumed. Life in the Near East was unsafe and changes were too great and too frequent for us to expect family records covering several centuries to survive. In the desert, especially under nomadic conditions, it is unlikely that family archives could be preserved. Thus, in general, genealogies were created not with a design to deceive but rather out of good faith combined with poetic imagination in order to provide a basis for maintaining family rights and privileges, preserving religious institutions and honoring family as well as national and religious heroes.

Purposes of Genealogy. In the ancient world, among Egyptians, Romans, early Hebrews and Jews in the age of Jesus, genealogy served several purposes. To understand the ancient world, its myths, legends and heroes, to know the national histories and people histories, we need to grasp the use of genealogy. Doubtless Jesus was the most important person to live in the ancient world or in any age. The message he broadcast to his disciples and his audiences, both friendly and otherwise, unleashed revolutionary ideas which have shaped the course and achievement of Western civilization: its nations, churches, art, literature and architecture. For us to comprehend Jesus' role as the Messiah, we need to know his genealogy and understand the use of genealogy for kings and priests in the ancient world.

First, one of the purposes of genealogy for every political or religious group was to identify the person by giving him or her a name. In the Greek world the practice was for a person to carry a family name and also to receive a first name. Among the early Hebrews names were assigned at birth or at the circumcision on the eighth day, as in the case of Isaac. The sources of names originally were limited; parents drew them from animals, such as Leah, "wild cow," or from plants, like Hadassah, which means myrtle. A child's characteristics often suggested his name, like Esau, who was a "hairy" person. Many biblical characters, however, are known by names which were probably applied in maturity. The names reveal what the person had become, such as "Savior" for Jesus. Names often sprang from events in the life of the nation, like Ichabod, "the glory is departed," or in the life of the family or of the father. Occasionally, names were changed by historical events, as when King Mattaniah took the name of Zedekiah under Babylon's regime at Jerusalem or when Saul's name was changed to Paul. Many persons noted in the Old Testament had names not of Hebrew origin, reflecting foreign tribes or nations among whom they lived. Joseph had an alternative Egyptian name, Zaphenath-paneah, while Mordecai was derived from the Babylonian name Marduk.

Second, in the ancient world, genealogy was used to indicate a blood relationship between individuals. Among the Hebrews individuals were frequently more descriptively identified by adding "son of" to the given name: "Joshua the son of Nun," or "Levi the son of Alphaeus." Sometimes a city name was added, as in "Jesus of Nazareth," or "Simon a Cyrenian." From time to time a person's occupation would be noted in the name, as in "Joseph the carpenter," "Levi, a publican . . . sitting at the receipt of custom," or "Simon the sorcerer."

Third, during the ages of David and Jesus, as well as today, genealogy was used to underscore and advance family pride. The long genealogical lists in the Old Testament, in Genesis Chapter 36 and in I Chronicles, chapters 1 and 2, and in the New Testament, Luke, Chapter 3, reflect the Hebrew concern to prolong the prestige of important individuals. The longer a family could bridge the decades and centuries with a family tree decorated with many names and, hopefully, with more than a sprinkling of illustrious names, the better. Of course, with this attitude about genealogy, it is likely that many pedigrees were creatively "amended," if not outrightly fancified.

Fourth, a genealogy also described what kind of person he or she was. For example, Julius Caesar, at the funeral of his aunt Julia, remarked, "The maternal ancestry of my aunt is traced to kings, the paternal to the immortal gods. For the *Marcii Reges* [her mother's family] are descended from Ancus Marcius; the Julii to which we belong are descended from Venus. Therefore, in our family is the sanctity of kings, who have supreme power among men, and the venerability of the gods, to whose power kings themselves are subject." At once Caesar in his eloquent oration genealogically magnifies and characterizes his aunt, himself and his family.

Fifth, genealogy gave the person certain privileges, either by law or custom, in his community or nation. Particular civil, religious and economic roles in society were determined by genealogy. Inheritance from father to eldest son was the basis on which claims to kingship, the high priesthood, the leadership of clans and "houses" (family lines) and property rights were established by descendants of the Patriarchs in Canaan. To be "chief of the fathers of the priests and Levites" (I Chronicles

24:31) was a distinguished honor. In post-Exilic times, since 540 B.C., genealogy was recorded with special care to line up claimants to the high priesthood, to reestablish property rights which had lapsed during the owner's absence in Babylon and to check the denationalizing processes due to mixed marriages. It was for a lack of "pure" Jewish background that Edomites, Samaritans and Galileans were viewed with a scornful eye by their Jewish contemporaries.

In Judaism the phrase "son of" Abraham meant "heir of," as well as one physically descended from Abraham. It was a phrase of privilege as well as description. As a son of Abraham, according to tradition, a Jew was an heir to the promises Abraham had received. Also, the phrase "son of David," originally meaning a descendant of David and a reigning king, came to stand for an office. For a person to be so identified meant in the popular mind that he was qualified for a unique role in the life of the Jewish people, that of a long-anticipated ruler.

Finally, a genealogy, either oral or written, might have the purpose of inspiring a descendant to pattern his or her life after a worthy ancestor. The accomplishments of earlier family members, clan leaders, military heroes, political or religious leaders were to stand as models for one's self and for one's children, and for one's children's children.

From the beginning of recorded history, five thousand years ago, people have been interested in the genealogy of their gods, kings and priests. Through the decades and centuries of early civilization, humanity orally passed from one generation to the next for the explanation of the roots of gods, kings and priests. The genealogical accounts not only described the origins of certain groups and family lines, but also their relationship with one another. The genealogies may often be intricate and inconsistent within themselves and in contradiction to their purpose. The desire and design to record the purity of a family's descent as well as its continuity gave rise to creative embellishment of the genealogical account.

It is against this background of Near Eastern interest in genealogy that we turn our attention to exploring the roots of Jesus. Biblical accounts from the Gospels of Matthew and Luke have certain common details regarding Jesus' descent as well as several important inconsistencies. On one hand, there is the suggestion of the activity of God in Jesus' supernatural birth, while on the other hand, through a series of unknown and unsung ancestors, Jesus is seen as part of the continuing links within the House of David.

II

JESUS' ROOTS
ACCORDING TO MATTHEW

Like the morning bugler heralding the new day, Matthew's Gospel begins by dramatically announcing the genealogy of Jesus:

> The book of the generation of Jesus Christ, the son of David, the son of Abraham.

Every listener and reader of Matthew's words, whether in a synagogue during the first century after Jesus' birth or in a church on the eve of the twenty-first century, is fascinated by the roots of Jesus. Matthew's list of ancestors stretches from the founder of the Hebrew people, Abraham, through Jacob, Joseph's father, to David, the second Hebrew king who made Jerusalem the religious capital of all Israel. It is a genealogy fit for the greatest man who ever lived and whose influence on the daily lives of men and women in every nation around the world continues today, nearly two thousand years later.

Reciting to ourselves the long list of Jesus' ancestors, Abraham, Isaac, Jacob and Judah and all of the others forward for thirty-eight more generations, we are reminded again and again of the long history of the Jews. Jesus' genealogy is indeed a brief history of Israel, a people called by God to be his people. Jesus was at once a prophet, teacher, Son of Man, Son of God, Messiah: His life and roots were entwined with the history and destiny of his family and his people. The pedigree of Jesus recorded in Matthew associates Jesus with the *rulers and ruling houses of the Hebrews and the Kingdom of Judah. It is a royal lineage.*

Why Did Matthew Write His Book? We should ask ourselves

why the compiler of Matthew, the first book in the New Testament, wrote his account of the "good news" of Jesus Christ. Written between A.D. 70 and 100, it has been a popular book for Christians since the early second century. It became prominent in the early church, probably at Antioch, a Hellenistic city in northwest Syria (today the city appears in our atlases as Antakya in Turkey). In the Greco-Roman world Antioch was one of the three cities of the age, ranked with Rome and Alexandria. It was an early center of Christian expansion and an important intersection for sea and overland trade in the Mediterranean world, Syrian countryside and the Eastern countries.

Matthew's book suggests the possibility that it was shaped by several years of preaching about the life and work of Jesus. Its rhythm and measuredness of story suggest a refinement which stems from repeated recitation. Based on an oral tradition of the first followers of Jesus, including the earliest preachers of the early church, this Gospel became a handbook for membership in the first-century church as it describes in a full way the life, work and teachings of Jesus. In its pages we read of the genealogy, birth, infancy and ministry of Jesus, and we cast our eyes on the accounts of Jesus' teaching, the Passion and his resurrection appearances. It presents the new message of salvation, the new law of morality and the new era of the new church.

The book has been assembled with great care and artistry as if crafted by a master carpenter. Every section of the twenty-eight-chapter volume is well-arranged, smooth-flowing and memorable to recount. It was originally written in popular Greek, "koine," the everyday language of the people, the common language of the Mediterranean world: a lively, fresh and vigorous dialect, a language at once of the people of the cities and of the countryside.

There are several purposes for Matthew's book of "good news." As a handbook its purpose is evangelical, describing the principles of faith of the Christian church and persuading the listener or reader to follow in the footsteps of the Messiah. It also has the theological purpose of alerting its audience that the long-expected Messiah, the anticipated descendant of the family of David, has arrived; that a new era has begun for men and women and that God's promises to his people have been fulfilled. The author of Matthew in the first century after Jesus' death tied his story to the prophecies of the Old Testament, linking Jesus with the expected Messiah. We should note, too, that the book has a third purpose; it is a history book with a special point of view. In describing Jesus' life and work, Matthew calls to our attention that through Jesus, as God's instrument, God has acted in history in the daily lives of people. This interpretation gives a divine purpose not only to Jesus' life and to the life of the early church and its members, but also to the life of Abraham, Isaac and Joseph. The history of the Hebrews and Jews has a sacred plan, a plan known only to God from the days of their wanderings in the desert, through the powerful reigns of King David and King Solomon, to the brokenness of the Jewish nation and community following the Babylonian captivity.

While all of these purposes are important to our understanding of the life of Jesus, let us focus our spotlight on Matthew's genealogy of Jesus. We have already remarked in Chapter I that many Jewish families, particularly after the Exile in Babylon (c. 538 B.C.) began to keep genealogies. Pure racial ancestry was a necessary qualification for holding a priestly or civic office. The "true Israel" was composed of families with this certain and pure ancestry, undiluted by mixed marriages with persons from other nations and tribes in the surrounding region. At the time of Jesus many people knew their ancestry. The New Testament writers, Matthew, Luke and Paul, note that Jesus was of the family line of David. Certainly the long-hoped-for Messiah, "the anointed one" according to the Old Testament prophets, was to be an heir of David and a son of Abraham. In Matthew the high point of Jesus' genealogy (see chart on page 18) is his descent from Abraham, David and the kings of Judah.

In this chapter we should note that we must concentrate our study of Jesus' ancestry on the details we are able to gather from Matthew's Gospel. It disagrees with Luke's account, and we will examine those differences in the next chapter. It is also at odds within itself, and we will discuss those inconsistencies. Nevertheless, these conflicting details do not overshadow Matthew's majestic story of Jesus' Davidic lineage. His genealogy falls into

The Roots of Jesus
According to Matthew 1:1-17

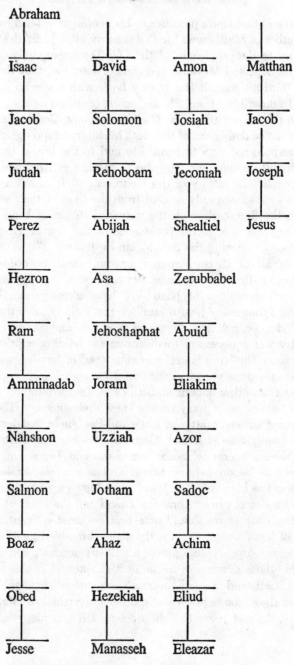

Abraham			
Isaac	David	Amon	Matthan
Jacob	Solomon	Josiah	Jacob
Judah	Rehoboam	Jeconiah	Joseph
Perez	Abijah	Shealtiel	Jesus
Hezron	Asa	Zerubbabel	
Ram	Jehoshaphat	Abuid	
Amminadab	Joram	Eliakim	
Nahshon	Uzziah	Azor	
Salmon	Jotham	Sadoc	
Boaz	Ahaz	Achim	
Obed	Hezekiah	Eliud	
Jesse	Manasseh	Eleazar	

three segments: first, from Abraham through the reign of David; second, from the rule of Solomon to the collapse of the Kingdom of Judah; and third, the Exile to Babylonia of her people, and their return from Exile to Jesus' birth.

From Abraham to David. The roots of Jesus, according to Matthew, are anchored firmly in the foundations of the Hebrew and Jewish people. Abraham was Israel's first great patriarch, and for Israel and Christianity he stands as the father of the faithful. His story, told in Genesis, is as wide ranging as his travels and touches many peoples and nations in the Near East. We do not know for certain the origin of Jesus' forefather, Abraham, but we have been hearing for two thousand years that he led a little group, perhaps only his family, from Ur of the Chaldees on the south bank of the Euphrates River northwesterly through the river valley to Haran, a city in northern Mesopotamia, now Turkey. Abraham settled in that city until he was called by God and promised land for his descendants. He journeyed from Haran through Syria into Palestine, to Egypt and returned to Canaan, the Land of Promise—all the while his faith in God's promise was being tested. Throughout his life the wandering Abraham, the "Father of many nations" and the "Founder of the Hebrew people," had come into contact with many peoples with a variety of cultural and religious backgrounds. Ur was an important city of the Chaldeans (Babylonians) in 2000 B.C.; Haran, of the West Semitic Amorites and Arameans; and Palestine, of the Canaanites, Perizzites and Hittites. After his sojourn among the Egyptians and his return to Palestine he met Hurrians, Elamites and five kings from the neighborhood of the Dead Sea. Through his son Isaac's wife, Rebekah, he was linked by his grandchildren with the tribes to the northeast of Nahor, the land of the Kings of Mari, while through his six sons by his second wife, Keturah, he was associated with six Arab tribes who lived in the east and south of Palestine. Abraham, whose friendship with God forged the special relationship between the Hebrews and God, is identified with at least ten groups of people in the Near East, people who are named in the description of land which God promised to Abraham's descendants.

Two or three miles from the city of Hebron, Abraham spent

his final days in the little village of Mamre. It was here, "by the oaks of Mamre," that Abraham erected an altar and later pleaded for the sparing of Sodom and Gamorrah. A few miles away, in the field of Machpelah, Abraham purchased a cave for use as a tomb in which he, his wife Sarah, and the other patriarchs and their wives were buried. The purchase of the cave signaled that Abraham was no longer an heir, but legally an owner of the land of Canaan. A portion of the patriarchal promise of seed and land was fulfilled. Today, Abraham's grave, because of its associations with the earliest days of the Hebrews, is a holy place frequently visited by modern-day pilgrims.

Abraham's towering achievements cast a long shadow across the pages of Jesus' genealogy: A complex, dynamic and vigorous leader and servant of his God, he boldly stands out as a giant ancestor. His second son, and his only son of Sarah, Isaac, through whom Matthew's Gospel notes Jesus descends, is, unlike his father the least significant of the biblical patriarchs. Yet, if he seems modest and insignificant, he is nonetheless the instrument through whom God works for Israel. Isaac was born under circumstances which prompted smiles and laughter: his father was one hundred years old and his mother, Sarah, ninety-one and well past the normal child-bearing age. But God had promised them a son of their own, and he kept his word.

We have only one account of Isaac's boyhood. It is a story familiar to us all: Abraham's sacrifice of Isaac, a story of faith and obedience. In "the land of Moriah" (traditionally located at the site of the Temple in Jerusalem) Abraham, at a command from God designed to test Abraham's faith, was about to kill Isaac as a human sacrifice when God intervened and provided instead a lamb for a burnt offering. The story emphasizes and echoes not only Isaac's obedience to his father's authority but also Abraham's faith in God. For Abraham's faithfulness he receives his son for a second time, and it illustrates again God's fidelity to his promise.

Matchmaking was as familiar to a biblical parent as it is for some mothers and fathers today. Abraham played the role of matchmaker for Isaac when he sent a deputy to the city of Nahor in search of a wife. At age forty, Isaac married Rebekah of the North Mesopotamian community and a relative of his father. For more than twenty years, they were childless, like Isaac's parents, and then had two sons, Esau and Jacob.

Because of a famine in the Negeb, one of the main regions of southern Canaan, Isaac moved to Gerar, an important city near the Mediterranean Sea south and southwest of the southern border of Canaan. Here he was on the one hand persecuted by the Philistines while on the other hand blessed by God with abundant grain, flocks and herbs. A peace treaty was established between Isaac and the king of Gerar, Abimelech, after the Philistines observed the success of Isaac's digging for wells of water. The occasion of the alliance was marked by the digging of a new well at Beer-sheba to which Isaac had returned. He also built an altar at Beer-sheba which bound Isaac and his family to the same God worshipped by his father.

When Isaac became old, infirm and blind he desired to give his patriarchal blessing and richest inheritance to his eldest and favorite son, Esau. However, the cunning and deceptiveness of his wife, Rebekah, intruded and caused Esau's twin brother, Jacob, to receive the benediction. It is a pathetic, shocking and tragic story of deathbed falseheartedness. The consequence of the unhappy incident was a long and bitter family feud. Jacob fled for a long time to the countryside of North Mesopotamia, fleeing from the land promised to him, while Esau, who now hated his brother, sought to kill him. They were later reconciled for the burial of their father, Isaac, who had died at the age of 180. The two feuding brothers buried their father in the cave at Machepelah where Abraham, Sarah and Rebekah lay.

The life of the third Hebrew patriarch, Jacob, from whom Jesus is descendant has been carefully portrayed in Genesis. He is much more clearly described than his father, Isaac, and no effort is made to overlook or whitewash his weaknesses. His story is one of conflict. Jacob was shrewd and crafty in both his personal and business life.

After defrauding Esau, Jacob fled to Haran, the city of North Mesopotamia where Abraham had lived and where many relatives still resided. He went to live with his mother Rebekah's brother, Laban, who agreed to give to him his beautiful daughter, Rachel, in return for seven years' service with his flocks. To this bargain Jacob brought energy, industry and property. His uncle's herds prospered. Laban, however, double-crossed Jacob, making him take as his wife the elder and less-attractive sister, Leah. Again he agreed to work seven more years for Laban for the hand of Rachel, and he kept his word.

During his long service in Haran, twelve children were born to Jacob. Of these, seven were from Leah, and two from Leah's maid Zilpah. The much loved Rachel, who was barren, gave to Jacob her maid Bilhah by whom two more children were born. Finally Rachel herself bore a child, Joseph, an answer to her prayer. The symbolism of the twelve children is important for us as we consider the historical and cultural associations of Jesus' roots. The twelve children of Jacob represent the twelve tribes of Israel, joined through the genealogy of Jacob, in parentage, allegiance and tradition.

After the death of his father, Isaac, Jacob remained in Palestine to assume his inheritance. He traveled widely and was associated, like Abraham, with many people: to Succoth in the Jordan River valley, to Shechem in the hill country of Israel, and Bethel, recognized as the sanctuary of God. His beloved Rachel died in childbirth on the road to Ephrath (Bethlehem) and was buried there. When a severe famine gripped Canaan, Jacob and his sons traveled overland to Egypt.

While in Egypt Jacob was reunited with his long-lost favorite son, Joseph, who because of his dreams had incurred his brothers' jealousy and they threw him into a well. After his betrayal Joseph was sold into slavery in Egypt where he rose to power and success in the house of Potyphar. Favored by the Pharaoh, Joseph became a ruler in Egypt and by wise planning saved Egypt, Canaan and his own family from the ravages of famine. Until his death, Jacob probably lived in the northeast corner of the Nile Delta, a region known as "the land of Goshen." His sons then returned his body to Machpelah where he was buried with Abraham and Isaac.

Jesus' ancestral ties, Matthew notes, continue through Judah, the fourth son of Leah and Jacob. The Old Testament tells us very little about this man whose tribe was to become one of the most important in the history of the Hebrew people. From the tribe of Judah came several other ancestors of Jesus: Boaz, Jesse and David.

Judah belongs to that first wave of Israelite tribes who migrated to and occupied the Palestinian hill country. The territory in which they settled was not large, a mountain ridge between Jerusalem and Hebron to the south, an area about fifteen or twenty miles in length and less in width. There were no old cities in the territory, and its trees needed to be cleared so the countryside could be prepared for farming. To the east was a natural boundary, the mountains known as the Wilderness of Judah, which was not favorable for settlement of either towns or farms. Expanding southward, the tribe of Judah became Great Judah, exercising political leadership and forging first an alliance of tribes and then a state. This expansion movement led to a further mixing of peoples and clans, peoples who were Israelites.

Perez, Jesus' ancestor, was one of the twin sons of Judah and Tamar. Tamar was the Canaanite wife of Judah's eldest son, Er, who was slain by Yahweh, God's own name, as punishment for his wickedness. Tamar remained a widow long after Er's death because Judah's second son, Onan, refused to marry her, as was the custom, and Judah withheld his third son, Shelah, beyond the promised time. Impatient, Tamar offered herself to Judah disguised as a prostitute and bore his twin sons, Perez and Zerah. In Matthew's genealogy of Jesus, Zerah's name is recorded along with Perez's.

It is not uncommon in the late twentieth century for compilers of family histories to encounter a problem or two regarding a relative who may have lived as recently as one or two hundred years ago. Particularly disquieting is the search for details about an ancestor, man or woman, for whom no surname is known. Jesus, too, had ancestors in this category. They may have been modest persons, farmers or shepherds, living in their tents and moving from one community to another as necessary. For example, we know little of Perez's son, Hezron, other than he was one of Jesus' kinsmen and that he led a clan of the tribe of Judah. He was the father of Ram, who is no less obscure on the pages of history. These persons, if they are remembered at all, are remembered because Matthew recorded their names on Jesus' genealogical list.

The giants in family genealogies stand up and stand out. It is the little people who are so difficult to identify. Ram's son, Amminadab, fits this pattern: He became the father of Nahshon, leader of the tribe of Judah, but we know nothing more about his life or family. We do not know if Amminadab lived in the country or in a city, if he was engaged in business or agriculture, or if he was a political or military figure among his people. Nahshon we know a little more about. He was one of the twelve tribal chiefs who assisted Moses in taking a census of the people of Israel during their wanderings in the wilderness. He performed other administrative tasks for Moses as Moses took his people, Israel, up from Egypt to the Promised Land. Nahshon, according to the lineage provided by Matthew, had a son, Salmon, who in turn was the father of Boaz of the family of Caleb.

Matthew's genealogy of Jesus identifies Boaz as David's great-grandfather and of the family of Hezron of the tribe of Judah. He was a wealthy and virtuous Bethlehemite of strong character, related to the family of Elimelach, whose daughter-in-law, Ruth the Moabitess, he married. From this marriage Obed was born, who became the father of Jesse and the grandfather of David.

The father of King David, Jesse, was a prosperous farmer and the father of eight sons and two daughters. He lived in Bethlehem and first appears on the pages of the Old Testament when the prophet Samuel makes a visit to Bethlehem to anoint one of the sons of Jesse in the place of King Saul.

Jesse is mentioned in the prophecy by Isaiah (11:1, 10) of the forthcoming Messiah: "And there shall come forth a rod out of the stem of Jesse, and a Branch shall grow out of his roots" . . . "And in that day there shall be a root of Jesse, which shall stand for an ensign of the people; to him shall the Gentiles seek: and his rest shall be glorious." In the Bethlehem Church of the Nativity, built over the cave site of Jesus' birth, a twelfth-century wall depicts Jesse's family tree and its many branches. Similarly, Paul, in his letter to the Romans (15:12) indicates that he saw in Jesus the fulfillment of Isaiah's "root of Jesse" prophecy.

David, like Abraham before him and Jesus after him, was

bigger than life. During the course of his colorful life he was a fugitive and a poet, a warrior and a religious leader, an able administrator and a talented musician, a king at Hebron and a great-grandson of the Moabite Boaz. David was a man of many sides, a dynamic and charismatic leader.

His rise to power is no less dramatic than his later career. Because of King Saul's disobedience during the Amolekite campaign, the prophet Samuel traveled to Bethlehem to exercise his duty to select Saul's successor. The story is a familiar one to us: Samuel, directed to the family of Jesse, invited them to a sacrifice, an important element of the Hebrew religion. After the purification and sacrifice, Samuel requested to meet the sons of Jesse, and he met them all except David who was tending to his flock that day. Yet, David was the person whom the Lord had chosen to be king of the Hebrews. So when David arrived from the countryside, Samuel "anointed him in the midst of his brothers" whereupon "the Spirit of the Lord came mightily upon David." He left home, according to this story, and became the personal attendant to King Saul at his palace.

Still another biblical story which brings David to our attention is the account of his heroic effort in killing the Philistine giant Goliath. It is the story of the conflict between the Philistines and the Israelites. Each day, the giant from Gath, Goliath, challenged his opponents to send one of the army of Israel to fight him. The army under Saul's leadership was tossed into fear and confusion. Meanwhile, David was sent by his father to take provisions to his three older brothers who were serving in the army. After his arrival at the army's camp, David heard of Goliath's challenge and accepted it. Appearing before King Saul, who warned David that he lacked experience and that Goliath had been a soldier since his youth, David expressed his willingness to fight the Philistine giant. As a shepherd, he had often battled with lions and bears that attacked the flock. Finally persuaded, Saul allowed David to fight Goliath. Choosing his own weapon, a slingshot, and without armor, David entered the battlefield. David's accuracy with a stone enabled him to slay Goliath, and the battle which followed led to the rout of the Philistines.

David now became a popular hero, and on every occasion that he entered battle he returned victorious.

King Saul, recognizing that the prophet Samuel had a curse upon him, sensed that his position of power was diminishing. He also felt that the old prophet and the young shepherd had fashioned an alliance. To protect his waning power Saul sought to push David out of the way. His wrath prompted David to seek refuge and safety among the Philistines, who were strong enough to protect him. His life became that of a wandering fugitive: from Gath to Adullam, to Mizpeh to Moab, to the forest of Hereth in southern Judah. Sought by Saul's legions, he continued his flight to the desert of Ziph, to Moon, to Engedia, halfway down the west shore of the Dead Sea. While hunting David, Saul fell into David's hands; but Saul's life was spared as David had sworn he would not lay hands on the Lord's anointed one. Again following the life of the fugitive, David returned to the desert of Moon and, not certain of his safety among his own people, he sought protection again from the Philistines at Gath. During his wanderings, David attracted a band of followers and at Ziklag he founded a small dynasty, which launched him in the path to obtain the throne of Israel. Roaming the southern areas of Judah, he wiped out his opponents, enriched his coffers with booty and organized his forces.

Learning of the defeat of Israel by the Philistines at Mt. Gilboa and the death of Saul by his own hand, David turned northward and marched to Hebron, nineteen miles south of Jerusalem. At that ancient city, once a Canaanite royal city, David was anointed king by the men of Judah. He was popular, powerful, political and divinely approved. Ever a diplomat and constantly positioning himself to acquire additional power, David, who was also Saul's son-in-law, was able to take advantage of the deaths of Saul and his sons, Jonathan and Ish-bosheth, to place himself in line for the throne of Israel as well. Representatives of all of the tribes of Israel traveled to Hebron and established a covenant with David and anointed him king of Israel. He was now king of Judah and of Israel: a united kingdom.

David's first step after becoming king of Israel was to move his residence from Hebron to Jerusalem. Jerusalem was an extraterritorial city, never a part of the kingdom of Judah or of the kingdom of Israel. The new king decided to smooth long-standing religious problems by bringing the old national-religious symbol of the Ark to Jerusalem, at once strengthening his ties with the priesthood and keeping them nearby under his watchful eye. This was an important step in unifying the two kingdoms and returning them to the earlier religious practices of the twelve tribes. Jerusalem became the Holy City, the place where the Ark, the sacred symbol of Israel, rested.

War and the pursuit of power punctuate David's reign, particularly during its early years. He fought the Philistines, Moabites, Ammonites, the Arameans and the Edomites. To Jerusalem David brought the riches of his distant conquests. He was the unchallenged ruler of the territory from Egypt to the Euphrates River. He was the king of Judah, king of Israel, king of Jerusalem, king of Ammon, king of the Canaanite states, which were part of Judah and Israel, the ruler over the Aramean states and Edam, and chief of Moab. In the early tenth century B.C., David was the most powerful man in the world. There was no strong ruler in Egypt, Mesopotamia or Assyria. David reigned supreme.

David was not without weakness, and he is best known for his affair with Bathsheba, another man's wife. In hopes of avoiding a scandal when Bathsheba became pregnant, David called her husband, the soldier Uriah, home from the front lines. However, Uriah did not want to remain at home while his fellow warriors were in the field. Accordingly, David sent him back to the front with the order that Uriah was to be placed at the center of combat. As a result, Uriah was killed and David was free to marry the widow. Nathan the prophet did not hesitate to call upon the name of the Lord for David's sin: that is, for taking the wife of another man after having him slain. David repented and submitted to the judgment of the Lord. Nevertheless, the baby died. Later, David and Bathsheba had another child, Jedidiah, who is better known to us as Solomon. The affair with the bewitching and beguiling Bathsheba signaled the beginning of David's decline from power.

If David knew all of the arts of warfare, diplomacy and political leadership, he knew precious little about the art of controlling his own family. The feud between his sons Amnon and Absalom over their sister, Tamar, ended in tragedy. Amnon, infatuated with his half-sister, forcibly seduced her, but his lust then turned to hatred and he sent her shamed and weeping from his house. Absalom sought revenge for his sister by having Amnon killed. Although crown prince, Absalom was exiled for three years to Geshur east of the Sea of Galilee. He was finally recalled to Jerusalem though not allowed at his father's court. Through the intervention of Joab, David's nephew and military commander, Absalom was reunited with his father. However, this proved to be a short-lived reconciliation, as Absalom proceeded to Hebron and proclaimed himself king in place of David. Army was pitted against army, and although David ordered his forces to spare Absalom that was not to be. Joab saw to it that Absalom was killed for leading the revolt. David's kingdom was bruised and scarred and remained badly divided. In the end it was David's personal charisma, rather than his political skills, which held together his wide-ranging empire: forty years as king of Judah and thirty-three years as king of Israel.

During the last days of David, Zadok the priest and Nathan the prophet anointed Solomon as king. Like his father, Solomon was a complex and many-sided man. He was an organizer and a leader, a builder and a merchant, a diplomat and a dreamer. In contrast to David's rise to power, Solomon did not fashion a coalition of popular support; nor had he had his leadership tested in conflicts against giants or at the head of an army. He succeeded to kingship because it was David's wish.

From Solomon to the Collapse of Judah. Through the reign of king David, Jesus' genealogy is presented in an orderly fashion and carefully told. It is at once a personal and patriotic story. The origin of Jesus, the Messiah, is interwoven with the oral traditions and stories of the lives and faiths of the patriarchs and of the nation. Israel's earliest memories as a people and as a nation, its moments of joy and its hours of sadness, are a part of Jesus' family history: His roots are among the ancestors of the Israelites, Abraham, Isaac and Jacob. These roots bridge Israel's history from a wandering, nomadic, Near-Eastern people to a settled, united, powerful and rich nation, chosen by God, under David's kingship.

Unlike his father, Solomon did not undertake any significant military campaigns during his rule as monarch. Although he did tend to defense needs by overseeing the building of a series of fortifications at strategic places in both Israel and Judah, his many achievements followed other lines and other interests. Under his administration was initiated a census of resident aliens in Israel, some of whom would be used as forced laborers on various royal construction projects. He also established a palace bureaucracy focused on internal development and not military operations. The nation was divided into twelve administrative districts with a prefect in charge of each. These districts cut across the old boundaries of the twelve tribes of Israel, thereby diminishing local power and attaching the nation more firmly to a central government in Jerusalem. The task of the prefects in each district was to see that the revenues were raised to meet Solomon's extensive building program.

The plans of the king required many people and an enormous amount of material. Solomon pressed forward with David's plans for the building of a House of the Lord in Jerusalem. He made arrangements with Hiram of Tyre, the Phoenician king, to supply cedar and cypress wood from Lebanon for this project. The Temple was completed in the eleventh year of Solomon's reign. Ceremonial festivities surrounded the removal of the Ark, the nation's symbol, from the city of David to Jerusalem and the most holy place in the Temple. The Temple was recognized as the dwelling place of the Lord, and when the Ark was placed within, it signified that the Lord had taken up residence in the house which Solomon had built. As the Temple was also a part of the royal palace, the Lord now dwelt in the king's house.

Outside of Jerusalem, Solomon's extensive building projects dotted the countryside: at Megiddo, where the legendary stables for 300 of the king's horses was built, there were also accommodations for 1,400 chariots and 12,000 horsemen; and at Ezion-Geber, a seaport on the Gulf of Aqabah, a great copper refinery was constructed. Ezion-Geber was a huge industrial complex of copper and iron smelters. The metal was not only shipped to building sites throughout the kingdom, but it was also exported. Known as the "copper king," Solomon's extensive shipping, mining and refining interests stretched from the Dead Sea to the Gulf of Aqabah and helped shape his diplomacy. He had to import raw materials for his industrial plants from nearby countries, requiring him to forge trade agreements such as the one with Hiram of Tyre. The reported visit of the Queen of Sheba was most likely a meeting to fashion mutual trading interests. While Solomon's extensive navy strengthened and supported his international business ties, significant trade was also conducted over inland routes, by camel caravans, crossing his territory and subject to paying Solomon his tolls.

The wisdom of Solomon is lauded in the Bible. He was a wise man with deep intellectual interests, and he surrounded himself at court with learned scholars. Adept himself at phrasing a well-turned literary proverb, Solomon is acknowledged as the Father of Biblical Wisdom Literature. We know, too, that one of the reasons for the Queen of Sheba's visit with Solomon was "to test him with hard questions," which he reportedly answered with ease. The book of Proverbs begins with: "The proverbs of Solomon, the son of David, king of Israel," and an extensive section of the book is entitled: "these are also proverbs of Solomon which the men of Hezekiah, king of Judah, copied out." "The Song of Solomon" is credited to his hand, as is the apocryphal book, "Wisdom of Solomon." It was a wisdom applied to the ruling process of governing his people, a wisdom to discern between good and evil. The Lord had given Solomon a wise and discerning mind, and all Israel heard about the "judgment which the king had rendered" and "that the wisdom of God was in him, to render justice." He was reputed to be wiser than "all the people of the east," wiser than the sages of Egypt, Canaan and Mesopotamia.

Jesus was right when he spoke of his ancestor, "Solomon in all his glory." His reign was indeed one of grandeur. As the nation's population grew, new cities and towns were founded, fortresses built, the Temple constructed and religion given a prominent place in the life of the people. Yet the labor and tax burden of Solomon's internal development undermined the economic foundations of the nation. The revolt of Jeroboam, of the northern kingdom, signaled the end of the power and splendor which were the hallmarks of the reigns of David and Solomon.

Popular discontent was brewing in Israel during the reign of Solomon. The prophet Ahijah, from the town of Shiloh, outspokenly opposed the dictatorial injustices of Solomon's rule and the allowance of pagan religious practices within Israel and called upon Israel to return to her special relationship with God. He understood kingship as a divine commission. Meeting one of the king's officers, Jeroboam, on a road outside of Jerusalem, Ahijah proclaimed the division of the united kingdom and Jeroboam's succession to the throne of Israel. The monarchy was to be wrested from Solomon's hands. When the news reached the king's ears, he acted speedily; but Jeroboam escaped to Egypt and remained there until after Solomon's death.

The last king to reign over a united Hebrew people was Rehoboam (c. 922–915 B.C.), a son of Solomon and Noamah, the Ammonitess. Anyone succeeding to the throne would have had at best a difficult time. Solomon had ruled as a despot, and accordingly there was much resentment among the people to his rule. His concentration of political power in Jerusalem at the expense of the old tribal network throughout the countryside particularly antagonized the people of the northern kingdom. His system of forced labor for the enormous nationwide building projects further eroded his popular support. It was upon such undercurrents of opposition to the government's policies and leadership that Rehoboam became king. Further undermining his inheritance, Rehoboam himself was not diplomatic or conciliatory toward his critics, declaring: "My father chastised you with whips, but I will chastise you with scorpions." This tough, harsh style of kingship prompted the peoples of the north to revolt. The united kingdom of David and Solomon was dissolved.

Prophets of both the north and south favored the rebellion. While possibly moved by the sufferings of the people, they were more concerned with survival and purity of the national religion, and they were determined to fight anyone who undermined it. The international alliances of Solomon had threatened the nation's religion by introducing alien religious and cultural influences. The empire which David had established, and which generations later would be viewed as Israel's golden age, an age of political power, could not be permitted to survive if the nation's religious mission would be compromised.

Fleeing Jerusalem by chariot, Rehoboam gathered together the people who were of the house of Judah and the tribe of Benjamin to wage war against the house of Israel in hopes of restoring the shattered united kingdom. The tribes of the north were loyal to Jeroboam while the southern tribe of Judah remained loyal to Rehoboam. Divorced and divided, both the northern and southern kingdoms were exposed to attacks from their stronger neighbors. Rehoboam proceeded to build fortresses throughout his kingdom in fear that the enemy to the south, Egypt, would launch an attack with its army against the now vulnerable and divided nation.

For three years the kingdom of Judah prospered under the leadership of the priests and Levites who arrived from the north where they had been deprived of their livelihood. When Rehoboam strayed from the law of the Lord, punishment came upon the people in the form of an Egyptian invasion. The king had been disloyal to his God. Pagan influences which flourished during Solomon's reign were continued by his son. The nation had strayed from her divine mission.

The son and successor of Rehoboam was Abijah, who reigned between 915–913 B.C.. His brief reign was marked by the continued border warfare between the northern and southern kingdoms which had punctuated his father's years on the throne. He was followed by Asa as king of Judah (c. 913–873 B.C.) who initiated a wave of religious reform to purify the nation of religious practices to restore the worship of Yahweh to its rightful place. Yet, throughout his reign border warfare continued between Judah and Israel, and Asa fortified the cities of Judah to safeguard the approaches to Jerusalem from attack.

The Davidic line continued through Jehoshaphat (c. 873–849 B.C.), whose reign marked the end of warfare between Israel and Judah. In fact, the monarchs of the two countries entered into an alliance which was later sealed by the marriage of king

Ahab's daughter, Athaliah, to Jehoram, Jehoshaphat's eldest son—
an alliance which was to prove disastrous.

Jehoshaphat was an able ruler, bringing the country of Edom,
to the east and south of Judah, under his control and allowing
Judah to control the caravan trade routes from Arabia. This renewal of an economic tie with Arabian ports, first fashioned during Solomon's reign, increased the wealth of the southern kingdom. Jehoshaphat raised a strong army, fortified cities and
waged war against the Moabites, Ammonites and Meunites at
En-gedi. Also he carried out, among the people of Judah,
through certain of the Levites and priests, a teaching program
which was intended to instruct the people in the "book of the
law of the Lord." He personally set an example for the worship
of Yahweh in the kingdom. With his death the era of peace-
fulness between the kingdoms of Israel and Judah came to an
end.

We have already noted that Jehoshaphat's heir, Jehoram (c.
849–842 B.C.), married Athaliah, the daughter of Ahab, the king
of Israel. Under her influence, Baal worship—the fertility God of
Canaan—was encouraged. It may have been this diversion from
Judah's religious mission as God's chosen people which
prompted Jehoram to put to death six of his brothers. They all
were princes of Judah and while their father was alive shared in
the tasks of administering the government; however, their disap-
proval of their brother's religious waywardness doubtlessly triggered their deaths. Faced with revolt from within, most likely
led by his brothers and their followers, Jehoram's rule was also
buffeted by the secession of Edom and the reestablishment of its
independence, and from outside the country, the rise of Assyria
to the east. Libnah also sent its armies against Judah as did the
Philistines and the Arabs.

Jesus' genealogy is interrupted at this point in Matthew's record. Quite possibly the compiler, in writing this book, mislaid or
overlooked a note or two as he wrote. In any event, the reigns of
Judah of Ahaziah (842 B.C.), Queen Athaliah (c. 842–837 B.C.),
Jehoash or Joash (c. 837–800 B.C.) and Amaziah (c. 800–783 B.C.)
are not noted. But this was also a time of bloody revolution, first
in the northern kingdom, Israel, and then in the south, in Judah,

and palace intrigue and murder made uncertain who was in power. When king Ahaziah of Judah was slain by king Jehu of Israel, the throne of Judah was taken by the queen mother, Athaliah. She boldly and swiftly set out to destroy the royal family to eliminate anyone who could challenge her right to rule. The Davidic dynasty was in danger of being snuffed out.

No wonder that a revolt occurred again in Judah under the leadership of Jehoiada, the high priest of Yahweh. Backed by the people, the palace guard and mercenaries, he brought the young king Joash to the temple, crowned him and anointed him king (c. 837–800 B.C.). The queen, a despot and devotee of Baal, was taken by the palace guards and slain. Joash's reign witnessed the king's and people's renewal of their loyalty to Yahweh. Nonetheless, this was a period of turbulence and disorder in Judah. Joash was assassinated by some of his palace servants and succeeded by his son Amaziah. The most noteworthy achievement of Amaziah's reign was the reconquest of Edom, which had won its independence from Judah fifty years earlier. However, disorder and conspiracy continued to rule Judah, and Amaziah, like his father before him, was murdered.

Our genealogical record in Matthew does not mention the political and religious chaos in the kingdom of Judah for six decades. Instead, the author telescopes this bloody episode in the nation's history and indicates that Uzziah succeeded his father, Jehoram, in Jesus' line of ancestry. His reign was long (c. 783–742 B.C.) and prosperous, matching for the kingdom of Judah the splendor of Solomon's monarchy two centuries earlier. Uzziah strengthened his army, fortified his cities and frontier outposts and campaigned against his enemies. He invaded the territory of the Philistines and the conquered countryside, which allowed him to control overland trade routes, and directed his armies to Arabia for the same purpose, too. Stricken with leprosy about 750 B.C., his son Jotham served as regent for the last eight years of his reign (c. 750–742 B.C.).

Only twenty-five years old when he began to rule in his own right (c. 742–735 B.C.), Jotham continued the building efforts of his father in Jerusalem and in the countryside of Judah. Jerusalem's city walls were extended and the city was further fortified.

On the battlefields, his troops were victorious over the Ammonites. His troops rebuffed the attacks against Judah's borders of the armies of the northern allies, Syria and Israel.

Chaos followed Jotham's reign in Judah. The new king, Ahaz (c. 735–715 B.C.), Jotham's son, proved to be a vassal of Judah's strong neighbor, Assyria. Wary of an alliance with Syria and Israel to the north, who in turn threatened to seige Jerusalem, Ahaz sought the aid of Tiglath-pileser, the Assyrian king, who quickly sent his armies into Israel and Syria, conquering both countries. Assyria at this time lay within the boundaries of present-day Iraq. It was a military power in the Near East, and like the Greek and Roman empires, which were to follow, it was now prepared to flex its imperial muscles. Ahaz learned nothing from the fate which befell Syria and Israel: He was never a leader, but ever an appeaser. He was quick to pay tribute to his mighty neighbor and quicker to introduce Assyrian religious practices into Judah. Tiglath-pileser III summoned Ahaz to Damascus and gave him instructions for the establishment of Assyrian religious practices. Ahaz had defiled his kingship and the divine commission of Judah, God's chosen people. The prophet Micah condemned Ahaz's Judah: Its courts were corrupt, its priests insincere and at the highest levels of government the ethical requirements of God were abandoned.

It was then that Hezekiah, Ahaz's son, became the fourteenth king of Judah (c. 715–687 B.C.). Unlike his father, Hezekiah was an able ruler and his reign was one marked by prosperity and progress. Led by the counsel of the prophet Micah, he launched religious reforms to eliminate Canaanitish cult places and Jewish idolatrous objects. While his interests may have been more political and patriotic in character than religious, it is difficult to separate these two strands in the life of ancient Israel. There was a cleansing and a sanctifying of the Temple and a reestablishment of the Temple cult, which were followed by a great celebration of the Passover.

Hezekiah was also concerned with strengthening Judah politically. He was involved in the struggle to maintain supremacy between the empires of Egypt in the Nile valley to the south and with Assyria in the Mesopotamian valley to the north. The Assyrian king, Sennacherib, attacked the Judean cities and Jerusalem in 701 B.C., awakening "a new" revelation of the nature of God in the hearts and minds of the Jews. The "angel of the Lord" intervened and a plague destroyed the invading Assyrian army. The troops withdrew from Jerusalem and the Jews viewed the experience as a national deliverance ranking with the earlier Exodus from Egypt and the Return from Babylon. The real question was whether the nation could survive if the Assyrian army returned again. It was the prophet Isaiah, inspired by Yahweh, who provided the royal and national faith to meet the crisis. But Hezekiah, a praying king, shared and echoed the prophet's religious spirit and brought to pass during his life many of the achievements of a national Messiah.

All of this work was undone by Manasseh, Hezekiah's son and successor (c. 687–642 B.C.). He reversed the policies of his father and embraced the practices of his grandfather, Ahaz, moving closer to Assyria. His reign, which proved to be long, peaceful and prosperous, began when he was only twelve years old. Manasseh is remembered by the writers of Kings as "the most wicked King of Judah": a vassal of Syria who allowed again the worship of Assyrian gods and the practice of divination in Judah. Although Manasseh may have preserved the nation, his actions undermined the state religion, the God of the Fathers of Israel. Meanwhile, the international politics of the region focused on the power of Egypt, Babylonia and Assyria, bypassing Judah, leaving the country free by oversight.

Next in succession, not only on the throne of Judah, but also in Jesus' genealogy, was Manasseh's son, Amon (c. 642–640 B.C.). Following in the footsteps of his father, he too was a worshipper of Assyrian gods, but mercifully his reign was brief, only two years, when he was murdered by his servants in his palace in what appears to have been a court plot. After the killers were put to death, Amon's son, Josiah, was placed on the throne.

The Davidic line, the royal house of Judah of which Jesus was a member, continues. Josiah ruled for more than three decades (c. 640–609 B.C.). The notable event of his years on the throne, and he was one of Judah's greatest kings, was the discovery during repairs of the Temple in Jerusalem of the lost "Book of the

Law," which we know today as the core of the book of Deuteronomy. Josiah also took in hand the task of collecting the old traditions of Israel from the time of the Conquest to his reign. It was a review of Israel's history of the nation's uniqueness as the chosen people of God.

The "Book of the Law" was used by Josiah as an instrument of religious reform: Idols were burned and idolatrous priests were ousted from their posts. Religion was centralized anew at Jerusalem, and he placed the Levites into positions of preference. His leadership lifted his people to spiritual heights which emphasized the ethical character of God, his love to man and man's duty to love God. The chronicler remarks that in this cleansed nation Josiah led the celebration of such a Passover as had not been observed "since the days of Samuel the prophet."

Josiah lost his life at war, in 609 B.C., trying to protect the region of Haran from the forces of Egypt, advancing to aid the Assyrians. He was slain at the battle of Megiddo and carried back to Jerusalem in his chariot for burial.

The Babylonian Exile and Return to Jerusalem. The death of Josiah was a rehearsal for the end of Judah, which occurred twenty years later. Turbulent power politics dominated and manipulated Josiah's successors. His son, Jechoniah, merely eighteen years old when he became king in December 598 B.C., reigned for only three months. He inherited a kingdom which was disintegrating with Judah's rebellion against the rule of the Babylonian king, Nebuchadnezzar. Taken captive, Jechoniah was deported to Babylon and apparently never set eyes on Jerusalem again. In 598 B.C. the capital of Judah was in Babylonian hands, and thirteen years later it was in ruins: its walls torn down, its buildings torched, and its adult male inhabitants herded together and deported to Babylonia. Only a stillness remained.

The Babylonian empire began to crumble by 550 B.C. and it was captured by the Persian King, Cyrus, in 538 B.C. An enlightened monarch who implemented a policy of encouraging national sentiment and local religious practices, Cyrus issued decrees allowing captive peoples to return to their native lands. The Jews were free to remain in Babylon or return to Judah.

By 515 B.C. the Temple had been rebuilt in Jerusalem and it

was dedicated amid scenes of joy and animal sacrifices. The Temple stood, not as a national shrine as it had before the Exile, but as a local cult center. Yet it was for the next five hundred years the focal point of Judaism and the common bond for Jewish groups scattered throughout the known world.

There was another loss to be borne by the peoples of Judah in the years immediately following the Exile. The Davidic line seems to come to an end. We know very little about Shealtiel, the son of Jechoniah and the father of Zerubbabel, the governor in post-exilic Judah under the Persian king, Darius I. His reign was one of anticipation: The prophets Haggai and Zechariah foresaw Judah's restoration to national power. As a descendant of David, Zerubbabel was the messianic hope to reestablish the Davidic kingdom, but that was not to be under him or anyone else. We know nothing of the final years of his governorship or of his death. We only know that no known Davidic ruler followed him in the governorship.

Following Matthew's genealogical line of Jesus, we know more about Jesus' distant ancestors, from Abraham to Zerubbabel—nearly one thousand years—than we do of his forefathers between the Exile and his birth, a period of about 575 years. In any event, we know that life in Palestine was not stable between the Exile and Jesus' birth: that the cities and countryside were frequently overrun by one army or another falling under the banner of this empire or that one. After Cyrus and Darius of Persia had cast their shadow over the land, they were followed by the Greeks and Alexander and the Romans and Herod the Great. The turbulence of the times, the divisions among the Jews, cast aside the gathering and preservation of genealogical records. The people did harbor one hope, however, that the Messiah would soon come.

Jesus' roots are ornamented with saints and sinners and strangers. The record as presented in Matthew concludes with a long list of strangers: persons about whom we have no further biographical information. They are remembered because they were ancestors of Jesus. From Abiud, the presumed son of Zerubbabel, to his son Eliakim, the line passes from father to son including Azor, Zadok, Achim, Eliud, Eleazar, Matthan, Jacob—Jesus' grandfather—and Joseph the Carpenter, his father.

Matthew's record of Jesus' roots is a dramatic story. At the time he compiled his book he understood that the genealogy was historically accurate, that Jesus was indeed descended from Abraham and David, that all of those begats were in place on his family tree. But the genealogy serves another purpose: It is an outline of the history of Israel. The major figures of Jewish history from Abraham to the Babylonian captivity are remembered, and in recalling the names of the patriarchs and kings the reader of the list is reminded of the historical episodes which surrounded each person's life and the life of the nation. It is a people's history.

At the same time, another plan seems to have been in the mind of the author when he set pen to paper to forever cast in permanent form the first century oral tradition regarding Jesus' ancestry: that Jesus was at once the final chapter of Israel's history and the opening chapter of a new and long-expected era. He is the Messiah, a Son of David and a Son of Abraham. For Matthew he was the royal Messiah, descended from kings.

III

JESUS' ROOTS
ACCORDING TO LUKE

> And it came to pass in those days that there went out a decree
> from Caesar Augustus, that all the world should be taxed . . .
>
> (Luke 2:1)

Can you recall a time in your life when those words were unknown to you? Quite possibly you first heard the opening sen-
tences of Luke's account of the birth of Jesus from your mother's
lips as a young child. Or perhaps it was your father, observing a
long-standing family tradition after dinner on Christmas Eve,
who read aloud from the well-thumbed family Bible the story of
the first Christmas, as his father had done before him and his father too. On Christmas Eve and Christmas Day church congregations everywhere recite Luke's majestical story of the birth of
Jesus.

The details of Jesus' arrival in this world are riveted in our
minds and imaginations: his birth in a stable because there was
no room in the Inn; the moving comments of Mary carried by a
donkey and Joseph on foot walking beside her as they journeyed
seventy miles through the Judean countryside southward from
Nazareth to Bethlehem, birthplace of King David. It is the story,
too, of humble shepherds caring and watching over their flocks
in the cold, who in the quiet darkness of a winter night are star-
tled and alerted by the words of an angel that a Savior, the long-
expected Messiah, has been born in Bethlehem. Leaving their
flocks and making their way to the manger in Bethlehem they
behold the baby Jesus and kneel down to worship him. It is a
beautiful story simply told: It announces to everybody, Greek,

Roman or Jew, the birth of the Son of Man and the Son of God. It is a story punctuated by dramatic prose and measured poetry. It is a story which both the school child and the adult remember and recite with ease, awe and reverence. For it is the story of a miracle, a once-in-a-history event, the birth of a King, David's son, the Everlasting Father, the Prince of Peace. It is a story which bridges the earthly power of Caesar Augustus, whose rule and reign gripped the Mediterranean world, and the eternal, unseen but all-knowing power of God made manifest.

Unlike Matthew's Gospel, which begins with the dramatic recounting of Jesus' genealogy, the genealogical roots of Jesus are sandwiched into a later section of the Gospel of Luke, Chapter 3, verses 23–38. This genealogy is introduced by Luke when Jesus at about the age of thirty is preparing to begin his public ministry. In contrast to the clarionlike announcement of Matthew, the family tree described by Luke appears to be inserted in a rather offhanded manner, almost as if it were unnecessary or impolite to mention one's ancestors:

> And Jesus himself began to be about thirty years of age, being (as was supposed) the son of Joseph, which was the son of Heli . . .
>
> (Luke 3:23)

Why Did Luke Write His Book? As with Matthew, we need to ask ourselves, "Why did Luke write his book? How did he come to write the Gospel? For whom did he write his account of Jesus' life and work? When did he put pen to paper and write his book?"

Luke seems to have had several complex but useful purposes in mind. First in the introduction of the Gospel, verses 1–4, he gives us a personal explanation for writing the book:

> Forasmuch as many have taken in hand to set forth in order a declaration of those things which are most surely believed among us,
>
> Even as they delivered them unto us, which from the beginning were eyewitnesses, and ministers of the word;
>
> It seemed good to me also, having had perfect understanding

of all things from the very first, to write unto thee in order, most
excellent Theophilus,

That thou mightest know the certainty of those things,
wherein thou has been instructed.

It is a task Luke had to do: He had to write his book in order
to preserve in some permanent form the eyewitness accounts and
oral traditions which were current at that time relating to the
life, ministry, trial, death and resurrection of Jesus Christ. The
Gospel of Luke is the fullest account we have of the life of Jesus.
No doubt, the Gospel reports stories which were circulating by
word of mouth throughout the towns and countryside of Palestine.

Luke may also have been transcribing the words of Paul as the
apostle preached to the young churches in the Mediterranean
world. According to the early church Greek Father Irenaeus
(c. 125–202 B.C.), Luke was particularly well-situated to do this.
Writing in A.D. 185, Irenaeus, a distinguished theologian and
late Bishop of Lyon in Gaul (southern France), remarked that
"Luke, the follower of Paul, recorded in a book the gospel that
was preached by him." But according to tradition in the early
church, that is during the first two centuries after Jesus'
crucifixion and resurrection, the Gospel was written by "Luke
the beloved physician," friend and companion to Paul. As one of
Jesus' most devoted followers, and a chief architect of the early
church, it was Paul who energetically, thoughtfully and systematically broadcast the message of good news to friend and foe
alike in Corinth, Ephesus, Galatia, Philippi, Thessalonica and
Rome. As his friend and companion, Luke doubtlessly put to
paper the words he had heard Paul preach in sermons many
times before audiences hearing the story of Jesus for the first
time as well as before church members who believed and followed the Messiah.

Another reason which possibly prompted Luke to write his
book was the hope of converting to Christianity some of the
members at the highest level of the government of the Roman
Empire. There was some interest in the church at Rome. We
know that the wife of Titus Flavius Clemens, joint consul in A.D.
95, was a follower if not a baptized member of the fledgling

church at Rome. Furthermore, Luke may well have had in mind presenting an account of Jesus' life, death and resurrection which underscored that the purpose and message of Christianity was not politically dangerous; and that the early church was not a subversive or troublesome faction within the empire. Like all institutions in every age, whether political, religious, economic or cultural, the church community had an urgent need to polish its image and purposes among its critics and detractors.

During the first twenty or thirty years of its existence Christianity was viewed as a Jewish sect by Roman public officials. They were unable to distinguish any difference between the new church and the age-old synagogue. For some time this attitude worked to the advantage of the Christians as they were allowed a freedom from restriction and interference by government officers to exercise their evangelistic task. However, as the church rapidly grew in numbers and expanded its outreach to cities and towns considerably distant from Jerusalem, it came under closer observation and restraints from Roman officials. Orthodox Jewish leaders and spokesmen sought to renounce Christianity, publicly declaring that they had no responsibility for the new church. As the distinction between the two groups came into focus and became better known to Roman agents, irregular and local persecutions took place against the Christians, such as those under the Emperor Nero at Rome in A.D. 64.

Still another reason motivating Luke the physician to write his book was his desire to support the opinion that the new church had taken the place of the synagogue as the true Israel; and furthermore, that since Jesus was the long-expected Messiah of Judaism, the new church was entitled under Roman law and custom to the allowance and protection that the Roman government had granted to Judaism.

Luke probably had a fourth purpose in mind as he wrote his book: to show that the message of Christianity was to all people everywhere and that it was a worldwide religion independent of racial lines or national boundaries. This theme is pointedly underscored in Luke's genealogy of Jesus which records Jesus' descent from Adam, the first man, the father of all people.

Finally, in the verses describing Jesus' birth, infancy and genealogy, Luke seems to respond to a fascination common to all of us; namely, to describe the family origins and family life of special persons. The members of the early church were no doubt eager to grasp any biographical details of the Messiah and his family, and to know the roots of the man who healed the sick, raised the dead and comforted the poor.

Before we move on to discuss specifically Luke's record of Jesus' ancestors, there is another point or two which should be mentioned recording the character of Luke's Gospel. We should note that biblical scholars the world over who have carefully examined and analyzed the language and literary style of both the Gospel of Luke and the Acts of the Apostles have concluded that both books were written by the same person with the same pen. Luke's Gospel was probably written during A.D. 70–80, and like the other New Testament books it was written in the popular language of the day, *Koine* Greek. It was the everyday language not only of the people living in Palestine but everywhere throughout the Mediterranean world. More than that, it should be stated that as a writer Luke was an artist, a wordsmith: The majesty, elegance and style of his pen propels our eyes and our reading of his book from the first verse to the last. He was an educated man, at home both in the Greek and Jewish world. His book is indeed a literary masterpiece.

Luke's Genealogy: From Jesus to David. When we compare Matthew's genealogy of Jesus and Luke's we notice several important differences. Matthew, in descending order, lists Jesus' roots from Abraham while Luke's genealogy ascends from Jesus to David to Abraham through Adam to God. The Luke list of seventy-seven names is therefore longer than Matthew's forty-one. The list of ancestors overlaps for three of the historical periods of history of the Jews, but even so Luke's record is more extensive, noting fifty-six names while Matthew lists forty-one. During the period before the monarchy was established in Israel, about 750 years between Abraham and David, both genealogies are nearly in complete agreement except for one prominent difference occurring in the names between Hezron and Amminadab. Matthew has listed the name Ram while Luke records Arni.

The Roots of Jesus
According to Luke 3:23-38

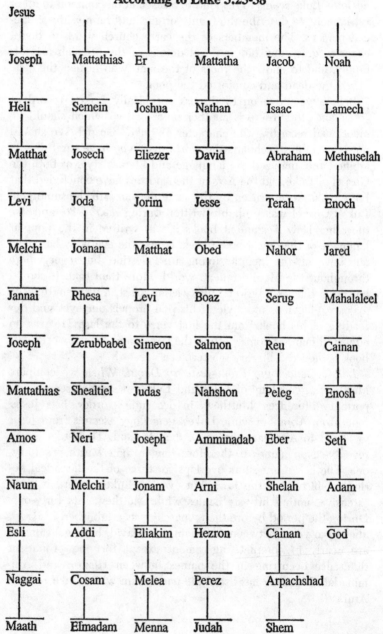

Jesus

Joseph	Mattathias	Er	Mattatha	Jacob	Noah
Heli	Semein	Joshua	Nathan	Isaac	Lamech
Matthat	Josech	Eliezer	David	Abraham	Methuselah
Levi	Joda	Jorim	Jesse	Terah	Enoch
Melchi	Joanan	Matthat	Obed	Nahor	Jared
Jannai	Rhesa	Levi	Boaz	Serug	Mahalaleel
Joseph	Zerubbabel	Simeon	Salmon	Reu	Cainan
Mattathias	Shealtiel	Judas	Nahshon	Peleg	Enosh
Amos	Neri	Joseph	Amminadab	Eber	Seth
Naum	Melchi	Jonam	Arni	Shelah	Adam
Esli	Addi	Eliakim	Hezron	Cainan	God
Naggai	Cosam	Melea	Perez	Arpachshad	
Maath	Elmadam	Menna	Judah	Shem	

The two genealogical lists are quite different for the monarchical period extending for four hundred years between the reign of David and the Babylonian Exile. In fact, the two genealogical records agree only on David, with Luke noting twenty-one names compared with Matthew's fifteen. For the 575-year period following the collapse of the monarchy and the beginning of the Babylonian Exile to the birth of Jesus in Bethlehem, Luke records twenty-two names while Matthew lists thirteen. The two records agree only on the first two names, Shealtiel and Zerubbabel, and the last two, Joseph and Jesus.

We know that each of us has more than one genealogical line: We have several on both our father's side of the family and our mother's side. In the previous chapter we discussed Matthew's design to indicate through his genealogical list that Jesus was of royal descent of the House of David. Luke has another purpose in mind: to show that Jesus is the Son of God.

Today, with so much interest being shown in the search for our own ancestors, we are naturally interested in Jesus' biological roots. A noted scholar, Raymond E. Brown, has explored this matter with skill and care in his important book, *The Birth of the Messiah*. He suggests that possibly Matthew invented his genealogical list, although this prospect is not a strong one as Matthew depends to a large extent on Old Testament genealogies for his list. If the list was to have any credibility with an audience of Jews, it is unlikely that Matthew would have fabricated a genealogical list, even partially. We have remarked earlier that the keeping of genealogical records and traditions became an important task not only for priestly and royal families following the Babylonian Exile, but for all persons who were concerned with establishing their rights and protecting their property.

It is quite possible that Matthew copied an existing record of David's genealogy. Since the House of David was the foremost Jewish family in post-Exile times, at least until the Maccabean age (c. 150 B.C.), it is more than likely that Matthew could have put his hands on such a genealogy. As the Messiah was expected by the Jews of Jesus' time, there were, no doubt, efforts to trace genealogically the royal and messianic lines within the House of David. However, we do not know if there was an official gene-

alogy for the Davidic line covering the years between the Babylonian Exile and the birth of Jesus, and that may well be the
reason that Matthew's list of Jesus' ancestors of this period is
briefer than Luke's record.

Another possibility for Matthew's list of Jesus' roots advanced
by Dr. Brown is the possibility that Matthew may have copied
the family records of Joseph the Carpenter, thereby explaining
why Luke's list of ancestors from Jesus to Zerubbabel is quite
different than Matthew's for that period. There has been a
theory discussed by many scholars that Matthew's record is of
Joseph's family while Luke presents Mary's genealogy. Yet, it
must be stated that it was not generally practical in Judaism to
trace a genealogy through the mother. Besides, Luke declares
that he is tracing Jesus' genealogy through Joseph's line of descent. Notwithstanding either of these views, most scholars today
dismiss the idea that either of these ancestral lists in Matthew
and Luke are in fact actual family records.

Many of the names on Luke's ancestral list are obscure. These
persons, if remembered at all, are recalled only because their
names appear in Luke's genealogy. We have no further personal
or biographical details for many of them: such as where they
were born, where they lived or the kind of work they followed.

Luke's genealogy of Joseph's family proceeds from son to father (rather than in the father-to-son manner as is the pattern in
the Old Testament genealogies as well as in Matthew's list):
Heli, Matthat, Levi, Melchi, Jannai, Joseph, Mattathiah, Amos,
Naum, Esli, Naggai, Maath, Mattathiah, Semein, Josech, Joda,
Johanan, Rhesa and Zerubbabel. Zerubbabel is the first name,
except for Jesus and Joseph, common to both the Matthew and
the Luke lists. We encountered Zerubbabel in our discussion of
Matthew's genealogy and remarked that not only was he the
governor of Judah during the reign of the Persian king Darius I,
but he seems to have been the last person in the long line of
David's descendants. Up to this point in our consideration of
Luke's genealogy of Jesus we have surveyed twenty generations,
from Joseph to Zerubbabel stretching across five centuries, from
the appearance of the Star of Bethlehem back to the dispersion
and Exile of the Jews under the invading Persian armies of

Cyrus in 538 B.C. and later under the rule of Darius. We should remember too that the prophet Zechariah referred to Zerubbabel as "The Branch," a descendant of David, and to him was pinned the messianic hope that in the political and religious chaos of the Exile the splendor of the Davidic kingdom would be restored.

Placed in Jesus' ancestral line Zerubbabel's father is recorded in both Matthew and Luke as Shealtiel, about whom we know little. The physician continues his list with Neri, Melchi, Addi, Cosam, Elmadam, Er, Joshua, Eliezer, Jorim, Matthat, Levi, Symeon, Judah, Joseph, Jonam, Eliakim, Melea, Menna and Mattatha, the son of Nathan. A subordinate branch of the Davidic family, Nathan was the third son of David, born in Jerusalem. His mother was Bathsheba, and therefore Nathan was an elder brother of Solomon.

Luke's Genealogy: From David to Noah. Luke and Matthew agree on Jesus' descent from David, the slayer of giants, legendary warrior and successor to Saul as the second King of Israel. His reign was one of power, purpose and prestige for the Israelites; a golden age of territorial and political unification and the establishment of Jerusalem as the holy city. For the King of Kings, the Son of Man and the Son of God, his descent from David was at once personal and symbolic as he was an heir of the House of David and therefore tied in the public mind to the achievements and traditions of David's reign, which was a beacon, bright and strong, in Israel's history.

There is little disagreement between Luke's and Matthew's lists of Jesus' ancestors between David and Abraham.

The genealogical line continues through Jesse, David's father, Obed, his grandfather, and Boaz. The roots of Boaz indicated that he was of the family of Hezron of the tribe of Judah. His father was Salmon the son of Nahshon, a leader of the tribe of Judah whom we have met earlier. Luke records that Amminadab, the father of Nahshon, was the son of Arni, a name missing in Matthew's list. Pressing on, backward in time, Luke notes next Hezron, Perez, Judah, Jacob, Isaac and Abraham, the founding patriarch. Abraham's father, Terah, a descendant of Shem was, according to Genesis, a native of the Babylonian city of Ur. Terah moved to Haran, where he settled and died at the age of 205. Terah was the son of Nahor whose life spanned 148 years. Serug was his father and the son of Reu of the family of Shem.

Reu's father, Peleg, was a son of Eber, the ancestor who gave his name to the Hebrew people. His father is recorded in Luke's list as Shelah the son of Cainan; although in the Old Testament genealogies Eber is identified as the son of Arpachshad (Genesis 10:24, 11:12–15, I Chronicles 1:18, 24). According to Luke's tradition of Jesus' ancestry, Cainan was the son of Arpachshad, the third son of Shem. Shem, in turn, was the eldest of Noah's three sons: Shem, Ham and Japheth. Shem stands traditionally as the name-giving ancestor of the Semitic people in general and of the Hebrews in particular. We are reminded that a Semite has been identified as a person belonging to those people of mankind either having common descent from Shem or speaking one of the Semitic languages of the ancient Near East.

Noah, Shem's father, appears not only as an ancestor of Jesus' family tree, but of everybody in the Bible. We all are familiar with the biblical account of the Flood and that Noah and his family were the only survivors. He is a genuine hero: his faith in God and his obedience to him protected Noah and his family from certain death. The son of Lamech, Noah was a ninth-generation descendant of Adam through Seth. His genealogy in Genesis records that he was born 126 years after Adam's death. His birth was the first after Adam's death, making him the second father of mankind after all other descendants of Adam were destroyed in the Flood. Like his descendant, Jesus, Noah has been called the "Bringer of a New Age," a messianic figure who rescued mankind from the chaos of the Flood.

We are told by Genesis that Noah lived five hundred years before he became the father of Shem, Ham and Japheth. He is remembered as a "righteous man, blameless in his generation": at a time when the world was "corrupt in God's sight." Consequently, when God determined to destroy "man and beast and creeping things and birds of the air" from the earth, "Noah found favor in the eyes of the Lord." The Genesis account tells us that God declared to Noah his decision "to make an end of all flesh," to "destroy them with the earth" and ordered Noah to build an ark of gopher wood. The ark was apparently a floating house not a sailing vessel, and was equipped with cells and covered "inside and out with pitch," in preparation for the impending catastrophe of a worldwide flood. The ark measured 300 cubits in length, roughly 450 feet, and was 50 cubits wide, nearly 75 feet, and about 30 cubits, 45 feet, in height and had three decks. According to the account in Genesis, it had only one door and one window. By applying our mathematical skills we can determine that the total deck space of Noah's ark was nearly 100,000 square feet, while its cubic content measured about 1,500,000 cubic feet.

Following God's command, Noah gathered his family and all the living creatures taken by him into the ark. Genesis notes that the flood occurred in the six hundredth year of Noah's life, and that one year later, "in the six hundredth and first year, in the first month, the first day of the month, the waters were dried from off the earth." Noah, ever obedient, awaited God's words to disembark and finally put his feet on dry ground seven weeks later, "in the second month, on the twenty-seventh day of the month."

After overseeing the landing of every creature in the ark, Noah "took of every clean animal and of every clean bird" and offered to God an extraordinary sacrifice of atonement. God accepted Noah's act of worship and said that he would "never again curse the ground because of man, for the evil of man cannot be put right by destroying him." Consequently, the regular rhythms of the seasons, the seed time and harvest, summer and winter, day and night, hot and cold, would not again be interrupted by a catastrophic event like the Flood.

Noah was a special man, chosen by God. He foresaw the Flood and he did something about it. He built the ark with time to spare and was prepared for the worst. Through Noah, the ark became a symbol of new hope, of a new beginning for mankind; and, it was big enough to shelter and safeguard all creation. It was through Noah and his family that the future of life depended. Only his family and the animals he gathered were saved from drowning, and given the opportunity to begin life on earth anew. Given the same command as God had given to the fallen

Adam, Noah was told: "Be fruitful and multiply and fill the earth." The Genesis story ends remarking that from Noah and his three sons "the whole earth was peopled."

One feature of the early biblical genealogies which captures our attention is the exceptionally long lives of Jesus' forebears. Noah lived for 350 years after the flood, dying at the age of 950. The life spans of Noah's father and grandfather, Lamech and Methuselah, were 770 and 969 years respectively. Enoch, Methuselah's father lived 365 years before God "took" him. Many cultures have similar traditions of long-lived persons, but to date none of the various explanations given for this phenomenon have proved satisfactory.

Luke's genealogical list of Jesus' ancestors continues, noting additional persons who lived long lives: Jared, Methuselah's father, and his father, Mahalalel, followed in succession by Cainan, Enosh and Seth, who according to Old Testament tradition was the third son of Adam and Eve. His father, Adam, deserves special attention as he is identified in Luke's genealogy as the "Son of God." At Seth's birth Adam was 130 years old, and he lived another eight-hundred-plus years.

These are descendants of Adam: little people and famous people, courageous people and weak people, but they have one common tie, they were a chosen people. The long genealogy in Luke provides a structure not only for the roots of Jesus, but also for our understanding of the history of Israel. God had chosen Adam and the people of Israel to be his people. There was a divine plan for choosing these particular people; it was not merely an accident of nature. God was seeking a people with whom he could make his covenant and through whom he would reveal himself. That is why the genealogies are so carefully presented. A listing of begats, whether our own or somebody else's, tends to be dull and meaningless. However, when we understand the purpose of the family tree and its personal details, our list comes alive and tells us a story, the history of a family.

Adam remains a key figure in Jesus' genealogy because Jesus was acknowledged in the early church not only as the Messiah, but also as the New Adam. Adam was the first man God created and from whom all mankind is descended regardless of race or nationality. He was made in the "image of God" and was blessed and given dominion over the earth with the command to multiply. The name Adam means "every man." The use of the name by the Old Testament writers is important as it suggests that their design was not to tell the story of one man, but the story of every man, a universal history of mankind. It is the story of humanity's history in the bright spotlight of God revealing himself to his creation. There is also a theological dimension to this story. We recall Adam's downfall: He disobeyed the command not to eat of the forbidden fruit in the Garden of Eden and was, in punishment, driven from the Garden. The theological significance of this story is that our sinfulness is related to Adam's disobedience.

The Apostle Paul frequently compared Adam and Jesus as he preached to his congregations. He spoke of the first Adam as like the "Coming One" because of the similarity in impact of each man's action on all of humanity. He preached that death became a part of life because of Adam's disobedience. Yet, Paul remarked in his epistles and in his preaching that the grace of God in Jesus Christ is far superior in being able to overcome the consequences of Adam's disobedience. Paul, with his lips and his pen, was thus declaring the contrast between Adam and Jesus, between the old and the new way of being. Adam is the source of death while Jesus is the source of life. The first Adam was a "living being, from the earth," a "man of dust," while Jesus is shown as a "life giving spirit," a "man from heaven."

The Role of Number Seven. Reviewing Luke's list of forebears, we recognize that there is a numerical organization to his genealogy. He symbolically uses the number seven to present the genealogy. The Old Testament provides us with several clues regarding the use of numbers by the Hebrews. The Hebrews were familiar with the four basic arithmetical functions: addition, subtraction, division and multiplication. They also understood the use of fractions. Numbers were used in taking a census of the population or in preparing an inventory of goods.

In Hebrew literature, as well as in literature of neighboring ancient Near-Eastern cultures, numbers were used for rhetorical and symbolic purposes. Many of the biblical uses of numbers are comparable to those in the older literatures of the Egyptians, Sumerians, Akkadians, Canaanites and Hittites. The number seven was of sacred interest among the Hebrews as well as among these other peoples. For example, in Egypt the deceased person was to be met in the nether world by seven cows and one bull while seven gods and seven serpents would give him audience. Isis, the Egyptian goddess, was accompanied to the Nile Delta by seven scorpions. The newly born child's destiny was told by seven Hathors. In magic, which was a powerful interest and influence in the ancient world, as well as medicine, the number seven was significant. Seven gods are appealed to in incantation. Holy oils and ointments were seven. The proper dosage of pills was seven, and seven stones were used in certain remedies. Multiples of seven—fourteen, twenty-one, forty-two, seventy and seventy-seven—were also important in both the Old and New Testaments. Luke notes seventy-seven names (seven times eleven) in Jesus' genealogy, while Matthrew mentions in 1:17 that he has recorded forty-two (seven times six); however he either skipped a generation or was a poor mathematician as he lists only forty-one names.

Another avenue for interpreting Luke's genealogy is to note that there are seven patriarchs from Adam to Enoch, and then seventy names between Enoch and Jesus. Luke has twenty-one names in both the monarchic and post-Exile periods, while Matthew has fourteen. In the period before a kingdom was established in Israel, Abraham is fourteen names before David (Matthew) and God is twenty-one names before Abraham (Luke).

The number seven was so important in the Old Testament that we can only briefly mention some of its uses. Important festivals, such as Passover and Tabernacles, are seven-day observances. The New Year, the Day of Atonement and Tabernacles all occur in the seventh month. The Feast of Weeks and the Jubilee were based on the square of seven. Seven runs through every aspect of the cult: Seven days is the period for the ordination of priests and consecration of altars; victims for sacrifice are frequently seven; the number of altars seven; the sacrificial blood is sprinkled seven times; and so is the anointing of oil. The furnishings and decorations of the Temple were sometimes in seven, and the seven-branched candlestick was the most sacred object next to the Ark of the Covenant in the Temple.

Seven had a special association with vengeance and punishment as well as angels. The ideal number of sons was seven. Seven-day and seven-year cycles are occasionally mentioned in biblical literature. Famine and plenty come in seven-year periods. The clear and tidy division of time between Abraham and Christ into three periods of fourteen generations as noted in Matthew is artful. The seventy-sevenfold vengeance of Lamech and the forgiveness of seventy times seven are intended as figures of speech, both implying essentially an unlimited number.

In the New Testament we read of a variety of instances of the use of the number seven, such as the seven parables and seven woes in Matthew's Gospel; the seven words of Christ as he hung on the cross; and the postresurrection appearance of Christ to seven disciples. It is difficult to state that these many uses of the number seven have anything in common. However, we can say that seven is a special number, and its symbolic use in both the Old and New Testaments reflects a sense of completion and perfection.

Son of God, Son of Man. Our search for Jesus' roots as outlined in Luke has stretched across the time line of history from the Inn in Bethlehem to David, Seth, Noah and Adam, to the Creator of the earth, God. Jesus was recognized by members of the early church as the Son of God and the Son of Man. To help us understand the meaning of the phrase, Son of God, we should consider the manner in which the Israelites and the Old Testament compilers and writers thought about God. After all, he was not only the first ancestor of Jesus but also of all mankind.

In the Old Testament world the kind of question we would have heard would have been: "Who is our God?" Not as is fashionable in certain intellectual circles today: "Does God exist?" In the classical world, in the era of the Old Testament, such a line of questioning was unthinkable. Furthermore, in that ancient time such questions would be asked as: "What is God's name?" The earliest period in which God's name seems to have been revealed to man was during the Exodus of the Jews out of

Egypt. The spelling of the name was probably "Yahweh," and its meaning has been much discussed and debated by learned biblical teachers and scholars. The word seems to mean "I AM that I AM," or more directly, he is the creator. Yahweh was the God whom the Israelites named in their prayers, in their oaths and in their worship. Places of worship were named after him throughout the countryside, and the worshipper trusted that God would hear and answer his prayer when offered in his name. We need to recall in the late twentieth century that the close tie between God's name and being can be understood only against the background of religious thought in the ancient world, as the name of God or even of his temple often held independent mystical significance.

For the Israelites their God was a personal God: a God of justice, love, grace, jealousy, anger, wrath, vengeance and righteousness. He was a living God participating in the lives of people and in the history of Israel. His pleasure or displeasure was expressed in the language everyone knew and understood. Throughout the epochs and eras of Israel's history, the God of Israel was viewed as concerned with the poor, the weak, the friendless, the little people who had nothing else to depend upon other than his righteousness. Consequently, life assumed a majesty and meaning unknown in other nations in the Near-Eastern world. Israel's God was accessible to the common people, whereas the pagan gods of other lands were not approachable. The God of Israel heard his people and answered their petitions and prayers.

God had selected Israel from all of the nations on earth to be his people. He led the weak and oppressed people out of Egypt and slavery and formed them into a nation. It was Yahweh who guided the war of conquest, and even during the years of the Babylonian captivity of Israel and Judah, God was at work for his purpose.

The Israelites interpreted historical events as fashioned by God. We may ask ourselves, "Why did God select Israel to be his people?" It is a question which is unanswerable as it is anchored in the mystery of God's grace. It is a question that cannot be explained; it can be accepted only on the basis of faith and thanks. After all, God had called on these wandering peoples as they were led by one patriarch after another from Mesopotamia to Canaan, reciting again to Isaac and Jacob the promises made to Abraham. Their election as God's special people with all of his splendid promises meant the Israelites must have faith in God's promises.

Very early in the history of Israel, God's election of the Israelites was deeply engraved upon their consciousness. Israel had been called by God for his special purpose, to be his great agent on earth. At times Israel did not understand God's purposes, at times Israel was disobedient; but the people were struggling to understand God's design. It was a struggle which created constant conflict between God and humanity, between God's will and human desires. These were the people of the covenant, chosen by God, responsible and obedient to him. This sense of a legal contract between God and his creation, forged and fashioned in a nomadic, patriarchal society gave meaning to the individual and the nation. There were special ceremonies and sacrificial rites to honor the covenant. To dishonor, disobey or reject the covenant with God meant that the special relationship would be broken and dissolved.

The God of Israel was first called *King* and *Lord* because he had rescued a people, brought them together as a nation and established them to him in a relationship like a servant to a ruler. It was not a forced arrangement. God promised to be their king and to provide them with justice, salvation and security from those who would persecute them if they in turn would answer and be obedient to his purpose. God gave Israel the law to keep order and peace within the nation. He chose leaders for special tasks—Moses, Joshua and the judges—and gave them the power to do their jobs. Later, because of necessity, God gave Israel the institution of kingship; the human king like the priest was to rule on earth as God's special agent.

God also called his prophets, who knew his heavenly desires and designs, and proclaimed them directly to the people and their leaders. The later prophets of Israel, Isaiah, Jeremiah and Ezekiel, spoke frequently of Israel's special relationship with God. They spoke of future days when God would renew his association with Israel with an "everlasting covenant," a "covenant of peace," a "new covenant" written upon the heart.

Second Isaiah describes a servant who was to be the voice of a covenant for all people and therefore the agent of their salvation. The new covenant was a gift from God which would create in people a new heart and a new spirit to receive it. This is the concept of the covenant which is echoed and trumpeted on the pages of the New Testament. The Christian, as a member of the new covenant, in the blood of Christ, becomes the true direct and absolute heir of the election promises made by God to Israel.

The idea of a Messiah in Israel was tied to the understanding of kingship. From the days of Saul and David the royal office was shaped to conform with the established theology of the covenant. The king was anointed with holy oil and acknowledged as God's Anointed (Messiah). The royal office was divinely created and its occupants were considered particularly elect. Joined with the election of the king, as in the election of Israel, were the divine promise and covenant. God would grant enduring power and stability to the throne; in return, rulers were expected to fulfill the purposes for which their office was established, providing justice and security for the people. Kings were not to use their power in order to violate the law of their office or their relationship to God. They could not claim credit for the law or violate it; they could only administer it in justice.

When rulers misused their office and were unfaithful to their blessing, the theology of kingship was taken over by certain of the prophets in Judah. These prophets shifted the focus from the current king occupying the throne to a ruler whom God himself would provide from among the Davidic line in the new age about to dawn. In him will be a mighty warrior, an everlasting father of his people, a prince of peace (Isaiah 9:6–7), outfitted with the spirit of Yahweh to rule the world according to the justice of God rather than of men (Isaiah 11:1–5). His name shall be "The Lord our Righteousness" (Jeremiah 23:6); under his rule Judah shall be saved, dwell in safety (Jeremiah 33:15–16), and be reunited into one kingdom under a new and everlasting covenant of peace (Ezekiel 37:21–28). He shall "be great" over the whole world (Micah 5:4) and "his dominion shall be from sea even to sea, and from the river [Euphrates] even to the ends of the earth" (Zechariah 9:10).

The Christian understands Israel's hope as finding total fulfillment in Jesus the Christ, a hope that is now genuinely universal. The pages of the New Testament were written after the fact: after Jesus' trial, crucifixion, burial and resurrection. He is the risen Lord, ascended into heaven and sitting on the right hand of God (Psalm 110:1). He is the king to whom all power has been given in heaven and earth, for he is really the Christ, the Anointed One, and the Son of God from the seed of David. Accordingly, the royal theology of Israel was seen to be fulfilled in him, for he was and is the hope of Israel, the intermediary of the New Covenant, of the New Age.

Christ's rule, however, is not from an earthly throne but from heaven. The messianic theology of Israel has been transformed, the kingdom is spiritual and universal in compass. Christ accepted the messianic faith of Israel but interpreted it by means of the suffering servant passage in Chapter 53 of Isaiah. God's king of the New Age is the suffering Redeemer. He was despised and rejected by people, yet he bore the sins of the world, was exalted by God and crowned with glory and honor. Hereafter, the inhabitants of Christ's kingdom are the children of Abraham by faith and adoption, heirs of the promises, and members of the new covenant. The early church affirms that Christ is key to the central meaning of the Old Testament, but it must be remembered that the Old Testament is the clue to Christ. The faith of Israel enables us to see that entrance into the kingdom of Christ cannot be found among the religious of this world, but only in the faith of Abraham's seed of which Jesus Christ was a descendant.

It was commonly believed among the Jews that the Messiah would be a descendant of David. This belief had its roots in the various books of the Old Testament. Luke, in his genealogy, places much emphasis on Jesus as prophet and Messiah. He seeks to strengthen Jesus' messianic claims by establishing his Davidic descent and extending the genealogy through Abraham, thereby bringing the life and work of Jesus into association with the ancient covenant and promises which God made with Abraham and his chosen people. Luke's account of Jesus' roots is different from Matthew's genealogy, not only in the details of the family lists but also in purpose. Matthew was concerned with establishing Jesus' descent from the kings of Israel and Judah, and his genealogy of Jesus was really a brief outline of the history of Israel. But, Luke had another purpose in mind: He extended Jesus' family line to Noah, to Adam and to God, bringing Jesus into contact with all humanity and finally with God himself. Outwardly there is a similarity between the Greek and Roman emperors whose family trees attempted to connect their genealogy with a mythical god or hero. However, this similarity is only superficial, as Luke's genealogy is tied to the Jewish tradition which rejected the royal line in favor of the prophetic. The genealogy of Luke is through Nathan, third son of David who is identified with Nathan the prophet. The rule of prophecy from the Old Testament is echoed in Luke's book, not only in his genealogy of Jesus but also in his account of Jesus' ministry.

IV

THE ROOTS OF JESUS
ACCORDING TO MARK

The beginning of the gospel of Jesus Christ, the Son of God.

(Mark 1:1)

From this brief introduction to the Gospel of Mark, we learn the secret about Jesus before the story of his ministry unfolds. He wrote about Jesus, not from the point of view of any biographical or psychological interest, but because he believed that in Jesus' life the Jewish hope that God would act in the everyday lives of men and women had found fulfillment. Mark and the early Christians saw in the life of Jesus the beginning of God's final intervention in history—to overthrow the forces of evil and establish God's rule. The early Church called this new beginning "the good news about Jesus Christ."

It is generally agreed among New Testament scholars that Mark is the oldest of the three synoptic Gospels—Matthew, Mark and Luke. It is also believed that Mark was one of the primary sources for the other two, since the outline of events as they occur in Mark is followed by both Matthew and Luke, and about two-thirds of the material found in Mark is also present in the other two. There is strong reason to believe that both Matthew and Luke had still another common source relating to Jesus' life and ministry; both of them record a considerable amount of teachings of Jesus in addition to the details noted in Mark.

Mark is the shortest and simplest of the four Gospels. From a historical point of view it is the oldest and the most reliable. Not only is Mark closer in point of time to the events recounted, but there is less interpretation concerning the meaning of these events than one finds in the other Gospels. While Matthew's Gospel is formal and stately, Mark's is brisk and full of life and action. While Matthew collects and recites Jesus' sayings, Mark directs his attention to the marvelous things Jesus did and to the places where he traveled.

Who Was the Author? It is uncertain who actually wrote the Gospel, but tradition weighs heavily in favor of Mark, an associate of Peter. Near the end of the second century there was a man named Papias, Bishop of Hierapolis, who gathered and transmitted information about the early days of the church. He tells us that Mark's Gospel is nothing more than the record of Peter's preaching material. Mark certainly stood close to Peter; so near to him, in fact, that Peter called him, "Mark, my son." Papias wrote:

> "This also the presbyter used to say: 'Mark, indeed, who became the interpreter of Peter, wrote accurately, as far as he remembered them, the things said or done by the Lord, but not however in order.' For he (Mark) had neither heard the Lord nor been his personal follower, but at a later stage, as I said, he had followed Peter, who used to adapt the teachings to the needs of the moment, but not as though he were drawing up a connected account of the oracles of the Lord: so that Mark committed no error in writing certain matters just as he remembered them. For he had only one object in view, namely to leave out nothing of the things which he had heard, and to include no false statement among them."

The name John Mark occurs frequently in Acts and the Epistles. John is the Jewish name while in Latin it is Mark. His well-to-do mother, Mary, had a house in Jerusalem which was an active meeting place of the early church. From the beginning Mark was brought up in the very center of the Christian Fellowship and probably often heard people recount their memories of Jesus. More importantly, Peter, disciple to Jesus, was probably a familiar and frequent visitor to the house. John Mark's second name suggests to us that he was a Hellenist, connected in some way to the Greek world. This would seem likely since he was a cousin of Barnabas, who came from the island of Cyprus.

The New Testament record also indicates that Barnabas was a companion to Paul, and that when they returned to Cyprus from Judea, having carried relief funds from the Antioch church to the famine-stricken Jerusalem (c. A.D. 46), Mark accompanied them. Apparently Barnabas had been selected by the apostles to go to Antioch to preach to Jews, Hellenists and Greeks. Once there, he became one of the leaders of the church, and as the work of the Antioch church progressed and expanded it was considered worthwhile to launch a missionary journey to Cyprus and the northern mainland. Mark seems to have been assigned the day-to-day details of the mission beyond Syria serving as assistant to both Barnabas and Paul. After leaving Cyprus and on his arrival at Perga in Pamphylia, Paul proposed to travel inland up to the central plateau. Mark for some reason withdrew and returned to Jerusalem. He may have returned home because he was frightened to face the dangers of what was known to be one of the most difficult and dangerous roads in the world, a road strenuous to travel and haunted by bandits. He may have returned to Jerusalem because it was increasingly clear that the leadership of the expedition was being assumed by Paul, and Mark may have disapproved that his uncle, Barnabas, was being pushed into the background. Or, he may have gone home because he did not approve of the work Paul was doing. Saint John Chrysostom (c. A.D. 347–407), an eloquent preacher and patriarch of Constantinople perhaps with tongue in cheek, or possibly with a flash of insight, remarked that Mark went home because he wanted his mother.

After Paul and Barnabas finished their first missionary journey they proposed to set out upon their second. Barnabas was eager to take Mark with them again, but Paul refused, not wanting to have anything to do with the man "who had withdrawn from them in Pamphylia." So serious was the disagreement between Paul and Barnabas that they parted company and, so far as we know, never worked together again.

For some years Mark disappears from the pages of history. Tradition has it that he traveled to Egypt and founded the Church of Alexandria. Whether or not that is true, we do know that when Mark reappears in the New Testament, it is in a most surprising way. We learn that when Paul writes the letter to the Colossians from prison in Rome, Mark is there with him. In another prison letter, to Philemon, Paul numbers Mark among his fellow laborers. And, when Paul is waiting for death and very near the end, he writes to Timothy, his close associate, and says, "Take Mark and bring him with you; for he is a most useful servant to me." Whatever their earlier differences had been, Mark had redeemed himself, and he was the one Paul wanted nearby at the end.

Mark also joined another early church leader, Peter, in Rome. The two men had been friends in the earliest Christian years in Jerusalem. After the deaths of Barnabas and Paul, Mark and Peter moved toward a closer association. Peter's words, "Mark, my son," show just how close was the spiritual tie between the older and the younger man. As Peter was writing from Rome, this forms another tie with the early tradition which noted Mark as writing his book under the influence of Peter's vigorous preaching. This tradition was voiced by the widely traveled and forceful Christian philosopher Clement of Alexandria, as well as on Papias' record which we have previously quoted, with Mark serving in some manner as Peter's interpreter.

While Mark may be an obscure person on the pages of history of the early Christian church, he is nonetheless an important figure who personally knew and stood beside such leaders as Barnabas, Paul and Peter. We do not know where Mark was born or where he died. We know little about him or his family, his home life in Jerusalem or his missionary duties in the company of Paul and Peter. We do know his heart and mind were touched and changed by Jesus' ministry and message. He was very much an Evangelist.

When and Where Was the Book Written? The Bishop of Lyon, in Gaul, Irenaeus, wrote about A.D. 180, "After the deaths [of Peter and Paul] Mark, the disciple and interpreter of Peter, himself also handed down to us in writing the things which Peter had proclaimed." Christian tradition has claimed that Mark's Gospel was written in Rome after the deaths of Peter and Paul. Irenaeus noted that Mark wrote his book after the deaths of Peter and Paul. Their deaths are linked by tradition with the persecution of Roman Christians by Emperor Nero in A.D. 64–65, and since the Gospel is addressed to a Martyr Church—one which had known and was expecting persecution—it was probably written between A.D. 65 and 70. It is likely that Mark recounted in his book the story of Jesus' ministry as he had heard the details from the lips of Peter, explaining the expressiveness and drama of his Gospel.

The Purpose. We must ask ourselves again the basic question which we raise about all the Gospel accounts: Why did the author write his book? What was his purpose? Like John's intention when he prepared his book, Mark did not have a master plan. He was not concerned with writing a history of Jesus' times or a biography of the Messiah. His primary purpose was to write a theological book for the young church. Mark was writing his book for a church which was meeting hostility from the rabbis, the synagogues and the Roman government officials. He was writing his theological book for a church consisting largely of Gentile members who were worshipping in the knowledge of the persecutions and martyrdom of the energetic apostles Peter and Paul. Members of the early church must have wondered if they too would personally face harassment, persecution and possibly death for their faith.

Mark's Gospel is neither a life of Jesus nor a biography. He does not tell us, as modern biographers do, the physical and mental characteristics of Jesus. We do not know how tall he was or how many pounds he weighed or if he had any distinguishing physical features. There are no comments about his temperament: Was he a happy, lighthearted, tranquil man or the opposite? We do not know whether or not he was married. Neither Mark nor the other Evangelists give us any details about the number of years and months of his ministry or of his age when he died; and there is not the slightest hint of the influence of his early family life upon him or of any development in his outlook or beliefs.

We should remember that a biographer writes assuming that his or her readers will be ignorant about the subject matter of his or her book. Mark, however, is writing for fellow Christians who were as familiar as he was with the story of Jesus' life. He had no need to "introduce" such figures as John the Baptist, Herod and Pilate or to explain where such places as "the wilderness" or the "Jordan" were to be found.

Although Mark was not a biographer, connecting together the various stories and groups of stories with his narrative, he provides us with a history. He tells of Jesus' baptism by John the Baptist, of his later ministry in Galilee, of some trips outside Galilee ending with a journey to Jerusalem, and such events as the entry into the city upon the donkey, the cleansing of the Temple and the scene in the treasury.

Mark's task was to tell his audience, whether listening to or reading his words, why Jesus had died. He attempted to answer a question which attracted the attention of doubting church members and contentious, combative critics: "If Jesus was the Son of God, why did he have to die on the Cross in the manner of ordinary thieves and murderers?" And more importantly, if God was a loving God, "Why did he permit Jesus to die?" Mark's answer to these questions are the underlying theme of his Gospel: Jesus had died because he himself chose to die and give his life "for many"; and because it was the will of God and had been announced long ago, it had to happen.

Like the other Gospel writers, Mark had still another purpose in mind when he wrote his book. He too wanted to prepare a guidebook, a catechetical and liturgical handbook, for early Christians so that those persons who read or heard his words might believe that Jesus was the Messiah, and that, in so believing, they might have life in his name. He was writing also for the church in Rome and for the mission to the Gentiles. Mark's Gospel was not meant for Palestinians but for an audience of Hellenists. The Christian community in Rome had been attacked, persecuted and martyred under Nero, who blamed them for the great fire which ravaged Rome in July, A.D. 64. There was no confidence among early church members that those brutal, bloody and fiery days would not return again. The members of the young church were faced not only with the danger and harshness of persecution, but also with the reality of losing their lives for their new-found faith. For Christians it was a time of turbulence and trouble.

Who Was Jesus? Mark, like John, was not concerned at any point in his book with the roots of Jesus but rather with who he was and what he was. While introducing his Gospel by describing the ministry of John the Baptist and Jesus' baptism, Mark focuses on the active life of Jesus, from the beginning of his Galilean ministry to the end of his natural life. He tells the story of Jesus from his baptism to his resurrection; at no point in the sixteen chapters of the Gospel do we find a genealogy of Jesus. Because Jesus is presented as a Servant of the Lord, there is no need for a genealogical record of his family. As the Servant of the Lord, he fulfills many Old Testament messianic prophecies such as Isaiah's: "Behold my servant, whom I uphold; mine elect, in whom my soul delighteth; I have put my Spirit upon him; he shall bring forth judgment to the Gentiles" (42:1). Mark sets forth Jesus with a strong emphasis upon his miracles, which points to his power as the Son of God.

Since the earliest days of the church, Mark's Gospel has traditionally been associated with Peter's view of Jesus. Quite likely the words of the book echo the themes Mark heard from Peter's lips as he preached to Christian gatherings. The simple everyday language of the Gospel, written in a rough, colloquial and sometimes ungrammatical Greek yet peppered with Semitic flowering, suggests a person who knew both Greek and Aramaic and yet lacked literary refinement. Thus, the author appears to be a Jew, writing in Rome for a Greek-speaking church. Mark thought of Jesus in several different ways, all of which provide us different perspectives on perhaps the most complex man ever to live and walk among us.

From one such perspective, we note in the first chapter of Mark, verses 2 and 3:

> As it is written in the prophets, Behold, I send my messenger before thy face, who shall prepare thy way before thee.
> The voice of one crying in the wilderness, Prepare ye the way of the Lord, make his paths straight.

It is at once a familiar and eloquent statement which poetically bridges the messianic hope of the Old Testament prophets with the soon-to-be birth and ministry of Jesus. Mark is quoting a pas-

sage from the Old Testament, from the Book of the Prophet
Isaiah (40:3). The words convey two messages: First they reflect
the belief in the early Christian community and church that John
the Baptist was "the voice of one crying in the wilderness . . ."
that he was the forerunner of Jesus who broadcasted to all who
would hear that he was coming. At God's designated time, John
makes his appearance in the desert of the lower Jordan valley.
He was a prophet in the Old Testament manner, like Isaiah and
Zechariah, who proclaimed the judgment of God and urged Israel to turn from its wayward path toward God and baptize
those who would confess their sins. Throughout the countryside
of Judea, and from Jerusalem, the people go out to John to be
baptized, as he fulfills his God-appointed purpose and prepares
all Israel for the coming of its Messiah.

We must also recall John the Baptist's ties to religious traditions and to Jesus' family. His father, Zechariah, was a priest of
the house of Abijah and thereby traditionally as well as symbolically linked to Israel's history and religion. Through his mother,
Elizabeth, who was also of a priestly family, John the Baptist
was related to Mary, the mother of Jesus. He lived in the wild,
open country of Judea along the lower reaches of the Jordan
River north of the Dead Sea, where he practiced his ministry.
Obedient to the words of Isaiah he lived in the wilderness,
dressed simply and followed a virtually pure diet. John the
Baptist rejected the crookedness of his time and strictly followed
the laws of Moses. He lived and preached in troubled times: The
"sons of Abraham" had been disinherited; the Promised Land
was occupied by the legions from Rome; the chief priests in the
temple had "no king but Caesar"; and their rulers, like Herod
Antipas, held office only at the pleasure of their Roman masters.

Long ago God had promised Israel its land and political sover-
eignty. The prophets and seers of Israel had proclaimed and
written of a day of judgment when God's anger would be poured
out upon the wicked and his promises fulfilled to the righteous.
It is these divine promises and sacred writings that constituted
the basis upon which the people's hopes were raised for the coming of the Messiah and the Kingdom of God.

Through the eyes of the righteous, who kept God's special covenant, those false Jews who had gone over to the side of the Gentiles, such as the chief priests and the supporters of Herod Antipas, had sold their inheritance for a "mess of pottage." They were like a "brood of vipers." In the Day of Wrath they would be baptized with a baptism of fire and be utterly destroyed. Their slackness in keeping the laws of Moses, as well as the presence of the Gentiles in the land, rendered life in the cities and towns unclean. The choices for the righteous were few in the days of John the Baptist. Some escaped the unclean and degenerate life of the cities and towns by withdrawing into the wilderness and divorcing themselves from dirtiness. Others banded together and remained in the towns and cities, maintaining their purity by complicated and highly refined systems of washing. However, the vast majority of Jews, either voluntarily or because of their occupations, were tightly entangled in the web of impurity woven into the fabric of political, economic and social life under Gentile occupation.

The wilderness of Judea was the center of religious hope as well as a place of refuge. It was rich in symbolism and tradition for the Israelites. God had dwelled with his people for forty years in the wilderness before bringing them into the Promised Land. In the wilderness the way of the Lord was to be made straight, and some believed the long-expected Messiah would first appear here. Later under the early Maccabees, Judea and its Temple had been established as an island of purity in a sea of Gentile sin. But by the beginning of the first century the tides of this sin had once again swept over this island until only the eerie wastelands of the Judean wilderness remained untouched.

It was in this wilderness that the Dead Sea Scrolls' community was living. They were preparing the way for the Lord's coming through study of the law and strict obedience to all that had been revealed to the prophets. United by a priestly discipline, the community constituted a "holy of holies" in which, through sacrifices of praise and perfect obedience, atonement was made for the guilt of transgressions, and for the purification of the land. Set apart in this way, the community served as a house of holiness for the priests and a house of community for the Israelites obedient to the law until the coming Day of the Lord. This day would be marked by the appearance of two messianic figures: an anointed priest and an anointed king for Israel.

Thus, the stage is set, and we can understand the excitement and enthusiasm which swept through the towns and cities of Judea with the news that a young priest, an Elijah, was baptizing in the wilderness. The king, the Messiah, would soon appear, and the Day of Judgment was about to begin. And so Jesus was baptized by his cousin, John the Baptist, in the Jordan River. John promised his audiences that he would be followed by one "mightier" than he, whose sandals he was "not worthy to stoop down and untie." Following his baptism Jesus remained in the Judean wilderness.

John had been active in distant parts of the wilderness. At one time he was east of the Jordan River near the main road running from Jericho to Transjordan. At another time he traveled northwestward into Samaria and baptized within a few miles of its more populous towns. Some who had been baptized by John were also active in other parts of the wilderness. John had started a movement, which, from the point of view of the public officials, was widespread and growing at an alarming rate. Through his disciples, John maintained contact with Jesus who was preaching in Judea. His question to Jesus was, "Are you he who is to come, or shall we look for another?" suggesting that John as yet had not surrendered his role as the guiding hand in Israel's preparation for the Messiah.

Again, we return to the question, "Who did Mark think Jesus was?" We need to carefully recount Jesus' deeds as described by Mark to know Jesus and his roots. It is through the events and conflicts of Jesus' life and ministry as remembered by Mark that we are able to understand his opinion as to the nature of Jesus.

Mark seems to have thought about the character and origins of Jesus in several different ways. We have already looked closely at the third verse of Chapter 1 of his Gospel to explore the role of John the Baptist in broadcasting Jesus' arrival and ministry. There is another side to that verse that gives meaning to the deeds of Jesus which Mark has chronicled in his book. The verse suggests the preexistence of Jesus before his birth in Bethlehem. Only a person who had come from eternity, who had been Lord,

could come to earth, to Bethlehem, at a particular moment and
become Lord. Mark thought too of Jesus as the Son of God, a
theme which can be traced through verses of the sixteen chapters of the Gospel. The notion is put forward by Mark (1:11)
when he recounts the baptism of Jesus at the hands of John the
Baptist: a Divine Voice is heard; "And there came a voice from
heaven, saying, Thou art my beloved Son, in whom I am well
pleased." This is a divine announcement as to who Jesus really is,
although not as straightforward or as precise as in the Prologue
to the Gospel of John, which declares that the Word which from
the beginning was with God and was God and in Jesus became
flesh.

The title of Mark's Gospel is "the good news of Jesus as Messiah and Son of God." He addresses himself to this theme during
the first half of his book, until the triumphant words spoken
when the apostle Peter answers Jesus' question "But whom say
ye that I am?" and confesses, "Thou art the Christ" (8:29). Then
the second half of the Gospel sets forth the story of Jesus' ministry of teaching and healing and thereby announcing to those
who would hear or read that he who was Messiah and Son of
Man was more than man, he was Lord of Man.

During Jesus' ministry there were all kinds of ideas about who
he was. His reputation had been broadcast far and wide. He was
great and mysterious. Even King Herod Antipas, who ruled over
the territory of Galilee and Peraea by appointment of the Roman
Emperor Augustus between 4 B.C. and A.D. 39, hearing wondrous stories of Jesus' teaching and healing, imagined that it
must be John the Baptist returned from the grave. Others were
saying that the great Old Testament prophet, Elijah, or one of
the other legendary prophets of the past, had come back to life.

While Jesus traveled with his disciples on the road to the
towns of Caesarea Philippi in northeast Palestine he asked his
disciples, "Who do men say that I am?" It is a mysterious, timeless question, not only about the nature of Jesus but also the nature of his mission. Peter alone among his disciples seems to
have found the words to answer, and he responded with a great
act of faith, declaring, "You are the Messiah." Peter had seen
mighty works done, but that did not prove that Jesus was the

Messiah. Jesus never said that he was "the Lord's anointed," nor had Peter heard the words which Jesus heard when he was baptized by John the Baptist in the Jordan. Although others may have thought of Jesus as the Messiah, only Peter dared to admit it. The term Messiah is a Hebrew word, meaning the "anointed one"; that is, one who has been recognized as king or leader by the religious practice of pouring over him the sacred, perfumed oil. The word stood for God's chosen and authorized representative in the work of restoring God's people to their true destiny, and thereby bringing in the kingdom and the rule of God. While Jesus does not firmly refuse the title Messiah, he tells his disciples to keep it quiet, a secret. Instead, he himself adopts the title, the Son of Man, the defenseless sufferer, who wins supremacy not by use of arms but by obedience.

Jesus is described by Mark in two ways: as a supernatural human being and as a man. He is the Son of God to whom witness is given at his Baptism and Transfiguration by divine voices; who is acknowledged by the evil spirits as their enemy and mutilator; and who is dressed throughout Mark's Gospel in works of supernatural power. He wears the clothes of authority from heaven; he knows the secrets within people's hearts; he ranks higher than the angels. As the Son of Man, he is the final judge who shall come "with the clouds." He has authority on earth to forgive sins and is Lord of the Sabbath. For Mark, as well as for all the Gospel writers, Jesus as Messiah is also the Son of God, who is obedient to God's will even to his death on the Cross at Calvary.

Mark writes of Jesus in a human way as truly a man. He notes that Jesus shared the same kinds of physical and emotional feelings which we meet in our daily lives or at crucial moments: He can be tired, angry and grieved; he can sigh and be moved by indignation; he can be "greatly amazed" and "sore troubled"; he is not all-knowing; he is addressed by his disciples with such familiar words as "Teacher" or "Rabbi." Mark's picture of Jesus harmonizes the view of a being who is both human and divine.

A final message that Mark also intended to convey to his readers was that the Jesus who walked among his people, who taught them and healed them, and despite his death on the cross and burial in a grave and resurrection, would come again. He would return at an unknown future time and usher in the final manifestation of the kingdom of God.

V

THE ROOTS OF JESUS
ACCORDING TO JOHN

In the beginning was the Word, and the Word was with God,
and the Word was God.

The same was in the beginning with God.

All things were made by him; and without him was not any
thing made that was made.

In him was life; and the life was the light of men.

And the light shineth in darkness; and the darkness compre-
hended it not.

(John 1:1–5)

The Gospel of John begins with words as powerful, dramatic
and spellbinding as any in the Bible; they are a unique blend of
historical fact with religious interpretation. As early as A.D. 200
Clement of Alexandria, the Greek-born theologian and catechetical schoolteacher, remarked about the difference in style and
content between John's writings and the Gospels of Matthew,
Mark and Luke: "Last of all John, perceiving that the bodily literal facts had been set forth in the other Gospels, with the inspiration of the Spirit composed a spiritual Gospel" (Eusebius, *His-
toria Ecclesiastica*, 6:14, 5–7). John's book is not a biography of
Jesus or a history of the Jewish people. It is a theological book, a
spiritual Gospel and the message of the book is Jesus as the
Word (Logos), the anointed one, the Son of God. It is a book
that is much more difficult to understand than the first three
books of the New Testament since it focuses on ideas and words
about the nature of Jesus and his work, which are both abstract
and unfamiliar to us today.

The words John uses to describe Jesus are indeed uncommon ideas to us whether seen on the printed page or heard from the preacher's lips. Yet, the words and ideas John expressed were popular expressions among the theologians and philosophers of his time in Ephesus about A.D. 95. The fourth Gospel was at once influenced and shaped by two important intellectual movements in the Near East: namely, the long-standing and carefully refined philosophical and theological ideas of both the ancient Greek and Hebrew teachers and writers. The age-old musings by humanity as to the origins of the universe, how it all began, of the nature of God, and of human beings, gripped John's attention and purpose. His understanding of such timeless themes was shaped by the writings and teachings of generations of educators, rabbis and philosophers.

Who Was the Author? We ask ourselves about the fourth Gospel: Who was the author and what kind of person was he? Was he a friend of Jesus? Did he hear and see Jesus teach and heal and preach? Was he among the crowd in the hills near the Sea of Galilee whom Jesus fed with five loaves of bread and two fish? Or did he see Lazarus rise from the dead? Was he a Jew or a Greek? Where was he born, and in which town or city did he live? Had he been taught by the rabbis, or was he a Jew who had been educated by Greek-speaking and -thinking teachers?

Unfortunately, little is known about him. There is no biographical directory of first-century authors and religious leaders to which we can turn for help. Nor did the author leave behind either on the printed page or in oral tradition, many descriptive personal details. Since the second century learned scholars have vigorously and keenly discussed and debated the authorship of the book, but the matter is not any closer to solution today, nineteen hundred years later.

In the early Christian church such important leaders and theologians as Irenaeus, Bishop of Lyon in Gaul (c. A.D. 125–c. 202), Clement of Alexandria (d. c. A.D. 215), and Tertullian (c. A.D. 170?–d. after 212) the Roman theologian believed that John, one of the twelve disciples, wrote the Gospel. These three powerful church Fathers lived far from each other in such distant geographical regions as Asia, Egypt and Gaul. Beside the great geographical distances, each of the three church leaders represented widely different traditions within the church. Nevertheless, they were in complete agreement regarding the authorship of the fourth Gospel. In the book the author is identified as the "beloved disciple" (21:20–24) who sat next to Jesus at supper. John, the beloved disciple, was the brother of James, another of the twelve disciples of Jesus, and both were sons of Zebedee by his wife, Salome. Like his father and older brother, James, he was a fisherman on the Sea of Galilee, and together with Peter and James, John was one of the three disciples closest to Jesus.

Why Was the Book Written? Doubtless, after reading the familiar straightforward, easy, biographical accounts of Jesus' life in Matthew, Mark and Luke, we raise the question, why was the fourth Gospel written? What was John's purpose in telling his vivid story? Plainly, he too wanted to write a handbook for early church members, a handbook that gathered between its covers the traditions of Jesus' life and ministry which had been circulated by word of mouth by preachers and early church members. When read or heard, John's book was intended to broadcast to the reader, listener, indeed to the world, that Jesus is the Christ, the anointed one, the Son of God. It was faith rather than fact that was foremost with John; he was concerned with historical events not for their own sake, but for their use in igniting faith in the hearts and minds of his audience.

John casts his spotlight on several key events in Jesus' life and ministry. Living in an age of miracle workers as well as belief in the supernatural, John recounts several of the miracles Jesus performed: the changing of water into wine at a wedding; healing the paralyzed man and forgiving the sinner; curing the blind man and raising Lazarus from the dead; and, finally, Jesus' death and resurrection.

The first three books of the New Testament mirror the public life and ministry of Jesus. John's book reflects Jesus' simple and plain teaching of his disciples and his controversies with his enemies, and thus we have two different word portraits of the man. Although the portraits are different in details and highlights, they actually complement and supplement each other. We need to remind ourselves again that it was not John's purpose to write the biography of Jesus; he wanted to write a book which was essentially theological and mystical from its opening sentence, "*In the beginning was the Word, and the Word was with God, and the Word was God . . .*" to its final eloquent words, "*And there are also many other things which Jesus did, the which, if they should be written every one, I suppose that even the world itself could not contain the books that should be written. Amen.*" The themes of the books are at once simple and complex, a blend of history, biography and doctrine.

The fourth Gospel was probably written between A.D. 95 and 105, a time when the early Christian community was under attack from without and within. During these years the young church was engulfed and assaulted by heresy regarding theological doctrine. Such conflict and controversy divided congregations and split leadership. The church met critics everywhere. First, there was the opposition from key rabbis and the synagogue. Second, there was a flourishing form of heresy called Gnosticism with the Gnostic tendency toward Docetism, which rejected out-of-hand that God had become man through the birth of Jesus. John answered the battle cry, not with sword or slingshot, but with the most damaging and bruising of arsenals—words. He sharply contested the differences of the philosophical and theological critics by eloquently recounting and defending Jesus' human nature. His book was planned to overcome the objections of critics and yet present Christian faith in a manner which would also gain the respect of the educated and cultured people of his day.

Where Was the Gospel Written? Scholars and teachers through the centuries have been concerned with the question, Where was John's book written? Most wise teachers believe that the book could have been written in three Near Eastern cities: Antioch, Ephesus or Alexandria. All of them were vigorous and vital cities in the Hellenistic world. Antioch, located in Syria, was the most important Roman city in the region; it was a large commercial center, a beautiful city with great temples, a forum and theater. It was in Antioch that the early followers of Jesus were first called Christians. Antioch was a center for Christian learning and played a key role in the theological controversies of the early church. Alexandria was no less important. Founded by the legendary Alexander the Great in 332 B.C., it was a focal point for Hellenistic and Jewish culture. Later Alexandria became a center of Christian learning rivaling both Rome and Constantinople.

However, the strongest case can be presented that the author lived in Ephesus. Tradition within the early Christian community links John's Gospel with that city. It was an important hub in the Near East with a large Jewish population, and the supposed home of a sect which honored and followed John the Baptist. Ephesus, located in what is today West Asiatic Turkey, south of Smyrna on the Aegean Sea, was a leading seaport and was an intersection of many streams of Hellenistic philosophical thought. Nearly six centuries earlier the well-born Greek philosopher, Heraclitus, practiced his scholarly craft in Ephesus and introduced to learned discussion the word "Logos," an idea which was to have an indelible impact on the character and theme of John's book. Ephesus was also the city in which Paul exercised his most fruitful ministry.

It was in Ephesus that the early Christian community met the sharpest opposition from the leaders of the synagogue, which led to lively debates for a century, extending from the ministry of Paul (d.c. A.D. 67) to that of the distinguished Christian philosopher, Justin Martyr (fl. A.D. 138–167). John became familiar with the many crosscurrents of thought in Ephesus, and he straightforwardly met the uncongenial religious and philosophical ideas which flourished in that city. He had come into contact with both the legalistic and mystical features of rabbinical Judaism; he encountered the stream of Judaism which had been Hellenized; and he met the distinctive ideas of Hermetism and Gnosticism. With his pen John set his sights on these enemies of the early Christian church, but he did so in a fascinating and clever way. He used his opponents' weapons in the controversy: He used their language and refashioned their philosophical positions to serve his missionary message that Jesus was the Logos, sent by the Father, God, to be the light of men.

Who Was Jesus? When we read the distinctive words and unusual ideas of John's Gospel we cannot escape raising the ques-

tion, Who was Jesus? Unlike Matthew and Luke, John did not
record a genealogy identifying the roots of Jesus. There is no
family tree or list of begats included in any one of the twenty-
one chapters in his book. There is no mention of Jesus' parents,
Joseph and Mary. There is no genealogical association by John
with the founders and defenders of the Jewish people, such as
the patriarch Abraham or King David, nor is there a link from
Jesus to Noah or Adam. Unlike Matthew, Mark and Luke, John
was not writing Jesus' biography, he was concerned with presenting a systematic and refined theological guidebook for early
church leaders and members.

John does provide his reader with a map which charts who
Jesus is and where he came from. John's map is a word chart, a
narrative, at once descriptive and theological regarding Jesus
and his origins. While Matthew's and Luke's genealogical accounts of Jesus have many points in common, there is no account
in the whole of the New Testament which parallels John's words
about the roots of Jesus. John begins with a Prologue, a long,
rhythmical poem which briefly sets forth the purpose of the book
and sets down in mystical and theological words Jesus' origins. It
boldly declares:

> In the beginning was the Word, and the Word was with God,
> and the Word was God.
>> The same was in the beginning with God.
>> All things were made by him; and without him was not any
> thing made that was made.
>> In him was life; and the life was the light of men.
>> And the light shineth in the darkness; and the darkness com-
> prehended it not.

These abstract and theologically complex words are John's map
for our understanding of who Jesus is. We must review, word by
word, John's hymn to grasp his understanding of Jesus' origins.

The Word. There are several important words in the Prologue
which help us to understand John's view of Jesus' roots. The
terms are Word, Life and Light. Each of these terms on its own
is important to our understanding of Jesus; together they provide us with a sweeping view of the nature of Jesus.

The first book of the Old Testament, Genesis, begins with the familiar story of Creation: "In the beginning God created the heaven and the earth." In a sense these words are echoed in John's clarion statement: "In the beginning was the Word, and the Word was with God, and the Word was God." Although John's words are not new to our eyes and ears, they are difficult for us to understand today. We need to ask ourselves what did John mean by the term Word? The use of the term *Word* in John is linked to both Greek and Hebrew philosophical practices. In fact, the Greek term for Word is Logos, and the two words are frequently used interchangeably to express John's philosophy of Jesus and God in his Prologue. The central idea of the Word (Logos) is that it connects God and humanity. It was not a word new to John but one with a long history of its own. It was first used by the Greek philosopher and teacher Heraclitus, who lived in Ephesus between c. 535 and c. 475 B.C. He believed fire to be the underlying substance of the universe, and that the world is kept in order by fire, and that the fire gives life to the world and this fire is named Logos. Logos is the power of order in the world and it is order. Heraclitus' thoughts swayed and influenced thinkers in Ephesus and elsewhere. The Stoics, learned philosophers and debaters in third-century-B.C. Athens, were followers of Heraclitus and developed an elaborate system of doctrines. In brief, their view of God was that he was everywhere in the world, was its vitalizing force, and was the law guiding the universe. All things developed from this force and they called this God, this law, this vitalizing force . . . Logos.

The use of the term Word or Logos was not just limited to various streams of Greek philosophical thought. In the Old Testament we note a theme called the Wisdom of God acting in the world, and in people's lives. There was also a very old Hebrew idea of the Word of God, which was at work in the world. Consequently, in several of the Old Testament books, the phrases, the Wisdom of God and the Word of God are occasionally used to express the same meaning. "The Word of the Lord" is an expression recurring throughout the Bible. It usually means the will or purpose or plan of God, made known to individuals, such as to Abraham in a vision; to Moses in the wilderness of Sinai; to

Saul through the prophet Samuel; or to the prophet Zechariah
during the rebuilding of the Temple.

In the Old Testament books the passage the "word of the
Lord" is most frequently used to describe the act of revelation:
God speaks and his prophet hears. To illustrate this point we recall that at the beginning or near the beginning of the books of
the prophets Jeremiah, Hosea, Joel, Jonah, Zephaniah, Haggai
and Zechariah, is the formula: "The word of the Lord that came
to . . ." meaning that God has taken the first step to speak to the
prophets and makes known information about the supernatural
and eternal order. All God had to do was to speak and his purpose for humanity and the world was accomplished. "God said,
'Let there be light,' and there was light." The "word of God" was
expressed through oracles, revealed laws, visions, spoken and
written prophecies and teachings, and events in history.

A book from Apocrypha, the Wisdom of Solomon, gives us still
a different use of the term Logos. Its contents were also
influenced and shaped by contact between the cultures of the
Hebrews and the Greeks. In the book the Logos is recognized as
the universal healer (Wisdom 16:12) and is said to have leaped
down from heaven, as a warrior, bringing God's commandment
as a sharp sword . . . "it touched the heaven, but stood upon the
earth" (Wisdom 18:15, 16). Without a doubt the writer had in
mind here that the Logos had become a person and had come to
earth.

We should pause a moment in our exploration of John's
thought to discuss the meaning of the Greek word *Logos*. It is a
term used to describe both "reason" and "word." We recall that
it forms a part of many English words and is used by us all every day in our conversation. In words like psychology, geology
and biology it indicates that type of reasoning known as science;
biology is the science of life, and psychology is the science of the
soul (psyche). When the term appears in either the Old or New
Testament it is usually with the meaning of "word."

Another person, like Heraclitus, who had an enormous
influence on Jewish and Christian thought was the Jewish philosopher, Philo, who lived in Alexandria between c. 20 B.C. and c.
A.D. 50. He was the first of the Hellenistic religious thinkers to

connect Greek philosophy with biblical religion, and he introduced the idea of the Logos to bridge the world with the creator
of the world, God. For Philo the Logos was the intermediary
through whom God acts and exercises his creative power in the
world. Retaining qualities of the Stoics' Logos and the Hebrew
Word of God, Philo's God is removed from the world and must
have a go-between to connect him to the world. At times his
Logos is divorced from God and independent of God because
God is so remote; at other times the Logos is simply the Reason
of God.

Building on this background John adapted the term Logos to
his purposes in his Prologue. We could translate the first sentence of the first chapter of John's book to read: "In the beginning was the Logos, and the Logos was with God, and the Logos
was divine." Clearly and simply John has stated that the Logos,
which is the eternal God, took flesh and became human. The
Logos is Jesus, he is the Revealer of God because he is the
Logos, he is the Son of God appearing as the Son of Man. He is
not the impersonal and remote God of Philo: The intermediate
Logos, which is neither God nor a mortal, has been replaced by
a Logos which is Both God and human. This clear explanation of
the relationship between God and his creation has become an
important feature of Christian thought.

The Word of God is the Word of God! It is God's meaning,
and consequently it is the meaning of the whole universe. The
Word of God has been made known in the two tablets of stone
on which was engraved, the Ten Commandments, the Law of
God. Now, as John tells us, the Word of God is engraved, not in
marble or granite, but in human flesh, in Jesus. The Word who
in the beginning created the earth and the heavens has now
created a man, a man who once lived with God but who now
lives among humanity.

What was shown at the beginning of creation was not Law, as
the Pharisees believed; not reason or thought, as the Greek philosophers and later the Gnostics were inclined to suppose; but
the creative power of the Word of God. John's emphatic declaration in his Prologue is the theme of the Gospel: The Word, or
Logos, began at the beginning; it is the creator and the giver of

life and light. The Word became man in Jesus as a demon-
stration of God's creative power and an example to all peoples
forever of that power. As the Son reveals the Father, so does the
Word made flesh reveal the unseen God. John's primary purpose
in his Gospel was to show that Jesus is the Revealer of God. As
we have noticed, philosophers and religious thinkers for several
centuries, whether Greek or Hebrew in background and learning, had been wedded to the idea that the Divine Word is the
Revealer, and yet they had not found it possible to link God and
humanity. The task became one of reconciliation between Spirit
and Matter, the One and the Many, the Infinite and the Finite.
The philosophers and religious thinkers had previously written
that the Word or Logos is the Revealer of God, while John states
that Jesus is the Word and that "God so loved the world that He
sent His Son."

Another aspect of the many-sided features of the Logos doctrine is John's reference to it as a source of life: "In him was life;
and the life was the light of men." As the Logos created all
things, all created life is an expression of its eternal life-giving
power. This is not an idea new to us from the pages of John's
Gospel. Earlier writings of the Old Testament reveal that the ancient Hebrews and the New Testament authors are in accord on
the topic of life. God is the living God who has life in himself.
Life is the gift of God and is maintained by God. That is the
God of Abraham, Isaac and Moses. God is at once the lord of life
and death. But we must be careful to distinguish between the
physical and spiritual life as well as the manner of the conduct
of life. Human life, the life of men and women, is the life of flesh
and blood. John reminds us that Jesus brought the true life to
light by dying on the cross for the forgiveness of humanity's sins.
His death was a godly act of forgiveness for the whole human
race, not merely for Palestinians or early Christian church
members, but for all men and women in all places and for all
time. God's gift to the world is "natural" life, while through
Jesus the gift of "spiritual" life is offered to all people. However,
a person must be worthy to receive the gift as it is not an auto-
matic present. With his understanding of life deeply rooted in
the Old Testament's view that God is life, John proclaims that

Jesus is the eternal "word of life" and had become man so that the people who by faith had identified themselves with him would share in his life. Through Jesus alone, to whom it was given by God to have a natural and a spiritual life, can people have a spiritual life and in this spiritual life, which is God's life, become children of God. The divine gift of Jesus' birth shows that the new life is not destined to be a special privilege for the few, say, kings and queens and priests, but rather as God's blessing for the whole of humanity, young and old, rich and poor, from every kind of national and ethnic background. Depending on belief in Jesus, "the life was the light of men."

Hand in hand with John's acknowledgment that the Logos is the source of life is the recognition that it is also the fountain of light. Throughout the Old and New Testaments light is identified with God and as a divine gift. People have no light in and of themselves; whatever spark is in them has been received from God. The ancient Hebrews thought of light as one of the original events of this world. They never distinguished between natural and supernatural light. Light is created prior to and separate from the heavenly lights in the sky: the sun, the moon and the stars. Light set the world apart from darkness and confusion. Dawn before sunrise was to the Hebrews an indication that God pursued a special goal in creating the world. The dawn of each new day signals that darkness will not last forever. The light is again God's gift. The use of "light" is firmly established in the Genesis creation story. God is the creator of light and darkness and he has made his covenant with day and night. It is God's design that light shall co-exist in the world, it curbs darkness and is powerful because it can restrict darkness.

The Hebrews understood light as a source of life, "being born," "being alive" and the "light of life." In the Old Testament "light" marks "salvation" or "rescue from danger" because salvation is God's gift. Also, the Hebrews recognized that light brings order to the world, the regularity of the daily twenty-four-hour cycle, dawn, day, dusk and night. Light, too, in the Old Testament is a wellspring of knowledge as it is through light that the things of this world are shown in their relationship one to another. The steadiness of the revolutions of the sun, moon and planets signals God's law. At once light gives people knowledge and guides them.

Parallel with the use of "light" in the Old Testament is the use of "darkness" or "night." The Genesis creation story tells us that in the beginning "the earth was without form, and void; and darkness was upon the face of the deep." Darkness represents the original condition of the world, associated with orderlessness, and revealing itself as bad luck, doom or curse and particularly death. For the early Hebrews light is the sign of God's nature while darkness indicates ignorance of God's saving yet demanding will and, consequently, the source of sin. As light has superior power, it illustrates God's purpose and reveals the true nature of darkness, passing judgment on it and delivering people from its influence. There is a difference, however, in the use of the idea of "light" between the writers of the Old and New Testaments. When referring to light, the Old Testament emphasizes the value it has for people while the New Testament underscores the believers' responsibility *to act according to the light given to them.* Light is a divine gift which may be lost if it is not used or if it is ignored. Humanity has been transformed, according to this view, by the power of God's gift of the heavenly light so that they become "the light of the world."

The light, the New Testament authors tell us, is now forever present in Jesus and in the Gospel through which the work of his light is endless. The New Era began with Jesus' birth in Bethlehem and it will never be followed by darkness. John proclaims that God's light shines to all, but that the rejection of that light is the devil's work and people are rendered spiritually blind and if unchanged, doomed. Writing at length on the topic of light, John declares that God "is light", that he is the source or creator of light, and that Jesus is the light of the world, God's gift to mankind. The gift of light through Jesus is tied by God through Jesus' birth. The coming of the light, which is Jesus, illustrates God's love. True life in the light, John tells us, requires keeping Jesus' commandments, especially that of loving one another. A person who hates others accordingly lives in darkness.

Summary. The Gospel of John is the latest and most reflective and interpretive of Gospel accounts preserved in the New Testament. John's Gospel reflects ideas and situations which prevailed in the Christian community toward the end of the first century of the Christian era. The purpose of John's Gospel, as he himself stated, was to show that Jesus of Nazareth was the Christ, the Son of God, and that by believing in him we all might have eternal life. This purpose was one which John had in common with the men who wrote the other Gospels, but his method for achieving it was different.

The central theme in Matthew, Mark and Luke had been the coming of the kingdom of God, and it was in relation to this event that an account had been given of the life and teachings of Jesus. The messianic character of his mission had been described in terms of the miracles he performed, his kindly attitude toward the poor and oppressed, his power to cast out demons and heal the sick, and his instructions concerning the way people should live in view of the approach of the coming kingdom. In the Gospel of John the essential theme is the divine Logos, the word which was with God and which was God. He begins his book by declaring Jesus' preexistence with God in the form of "the Word" or Logos. John says nothing of a supernatural birth. His Jesus is the Logos who became flesh, a human being who possessed actual flesh and blood the same as other people. The most significant fact about Jesus, however, was that the divine Logos was present in him, and all the wondrous things he did were accomplished by virtue of the power of God. It is in this manner that John understands the relationship between the divine and the human. As God was present in Jesus, it was appropriate to refer to him as the Son of God who was the Son of Man. John's Jesus was not a baby born in a manger in Bethlehem and wrapped in blankets; his Jesus was the Logos, the eternal Son, the "only begotten" from the Father.

Thus, the Fourth Gospel served as a handbook in reinterpreting the faith in words that a new age and a Hellenistic world would understand. At a time when the ties with Judaism and the synagogue were broken, and many Gentiles had come into the church, John transplanted the Gospel of Jesus into Greek soil. He takes the ancient Hebrew idea of a personal God, illuminated by the life and ministry of Jesus and by nearly one hundred years of

Christian experience, and vigorously interprets it in the language of Greek philosophy. Jewish, Christian and Alexandrian Greek influences converge in the idea of the Logos, and thereby John was able to present the idea to a far-flung church accommodating a variety of traditions. Jesus is at once a historical person, the Son of Man, but also the Son of God, the eternal Father.

VI

THE HOUSE OF DAVID:
BLOODLINES AND DYNASTY

Then all Israel gathered themselves to David unto Hebron, saying, Behold, we are thy bone and thy flesh.

And moreover in time past, even when Saul was king, thou wast he that leddest out and broughtest in Israel; and the LORD thy God said unto thee, Thou shalt feed my people Israel, and thou shalt be ruler over my people Israel.

Therefore came all the elders of Israel to the king at Hebron; and David made a covenant with them in Hebron before the LORD; and they anointed David king over Israel, according to the word of the LORD by Samuel.

(I Chronicles 11:1–3)

Many of the descriptive and colorful passages in the Old Testament tell the story of David, the second king of the ancient Hebrews (c. 1000–962 B.C.). Youngest of eight sons of Jesse, a Judean farmer of Bethlehem, he was from the land, a shepherd boy, doing the most menial of tasks. Summoned and anointed by the prophet Samuel to join the court of King Saul, David in time became the symbol of his nation and of his people. We have learned much about David from the biblical accounts. He is at once one of the most human and frail of Old Testament figures, a person who makes mistakes, learns from his errors and then moves forward again. He is also a person who is bold, courageous and loyal to his God, Yahweh.

David was a brave captain in battle, a warrior who slew the giant Goliath and routed the enemy Philistines. Loyal to his mad king, Saul, David placed his faithfulness to the state above his

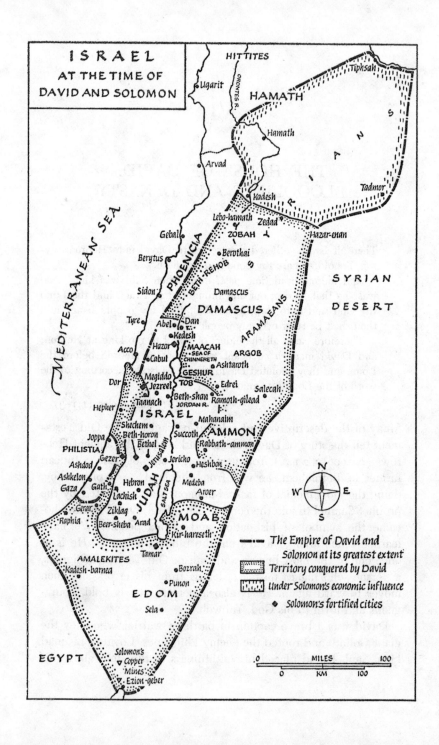

ISRAEL
AT THE TIME OF
DAVID AND SOLOMON

HITTITES

MEDITERRANEAN SEA

Ugarit

HAMATH

Tiphsah

ORONTES R.

Hamath

Arvad

Tadmor

Kadesh

A R A M A E A N S

Lebo-hamath   Zedad
ZOBAH   Hazar-enan
Gebal
Berothai

Berytus   BETH-REHOB

SYRIAN
DESERT

PHOENICIA

Sidon   Damascus

DAMASCUS

Tyre   Abel   Dan
Kedesh   T.
Acco   Hazor   MAACAH
Cabul   SEA OF
CHINNERETH   Ashtaroth
Megiddo   GESHUR
Dor   Jezreel   TOB
Taanach   Beth-shan   Edrei
Hepher   JORDAN R.   Ramoth-gilead   Salecah
ISRAEL
Shechem   Mahanaim
Joppa   Beth-horon   Succoth   AMMON
PHILISTIA   Bethel   Rabbath-ammon
Gezer   Jerusalem
Ashdod   Jericho   Heshbon
Ashkelon   Hebron   Medeba
Gaza   Gath   JUDAH   Aroer
Gerar   Lachish   SALT SEA
Raphia   Ziklag   Beer-sheba   Arad   MOAB
Kir-hareseth
AMALEKITES   Tamar
Kadesh-barnea   Bozrah
Punon
EDOM
Sela

ARGOB

N
W   E
S

——·—— The Empire of David and
          Solomon at its greatest extent
:::::::::: Territory conquered by David
▥▥▥▥ Under Solomon's economic influence
◆ Solomon's fortified cities

EGYPT

Solomon's
Copper
Mines
Ezion-geber

0   MILES   100
0   KM   100

own well-being. His friendship with Saul's son, Jonathan, transcended ambition and jealousy and served as a symbol of mutual admiration and trust. Successor to Saul as king, David was anointed as monarch by representatives of Israel's clans and tribes at Hebron. The common country shepherd boy, soldier, servant of kings and princes, national hero, outlaw, deserter and mercenary was now king by overwhelming popular support.

As dynamic at leading affairs of state as he was at leading forces on the battlefield, David fashioned the Twelve Tribes of Judah and Israel into a united national monarchy. He made Jerusalem, long associated with the nation's legendary patriarchs, his place of residence. The Ark of the Covenant, which held the holiest relics of the Israelites, the tablets of the Ten Commandments brought by Moses from Mount Sinai, was carried to a new resting place in Jerusalem. This act made the city holy, and Jerusalem throughout the ages would now serve as a permanent monument to David's genius and an eternal center for the Jewish people, the City of David.

King David became for his people not only a model monarch but also the greatest and most revered of their national heroes. His reign marked the transformation of the Hebrews from a rude confederation of tribes to a robust and dynamic national state. David's years on the throne lived on in the hearts and minds of his people and of their children and their children's children as the proudest moment of their history and the prophetic ideal of future glory.

After David had brought the Ark to Jerusalem, the prophet Nathan had a vision and told the king of Yahweh's promise: "And thine house and thy kingdom shall be established for ever before thee: thy throne shall be established for ever" (II Samuel 7:16). The prophet had promised that David's descendants would rule without end over Israel, and that they would enjoy a special relationship with their God. Solomon, second son of David and Bathsheba, succeeded his father to the throne, and with his accession the first link was forged for the establishment of the House of David to reign for eternity.

We know David's family lineage is complicated and needs to be understood against the background and circumstances of his

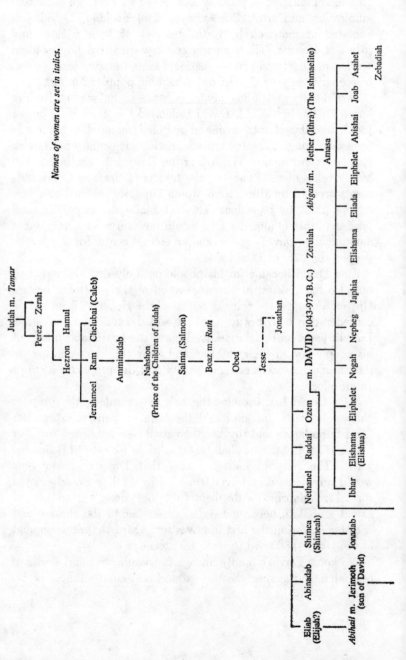

GENEALOGICAL CHART OF THE HOUSE OF DAVID

Names of women are set in italics.

Judah m. *Tamar*

Perez — Zerah

Hezron — Hamul

Jerahmeel — Ram — Chelubai (Caleb)

Amminadab

Nahshon
(Prince of the Children of Judah)

Salma (Salmon)

Boaz m. *Ruth*

Obed

Jesse ---- Jonathan

Eliab (Elijah?) — Abinadab — Shimea (Shimeah) — Nethanel — Raddai — Ozem — m. DAVID (1043-973 B.C.)

Abihail m. Jerimoth (son of David)

Jonadab

Ibhar — Elishama (Elishua) — Eliphelet — Nogah — Nepheg — Japhia — Elishama — Eliada — Eliphelet

Zeruiah

Abigail m. Jether (Ithra) (The Ishmaelite)

Amasa

Abishai — Joab — Asahel

Zebadiah

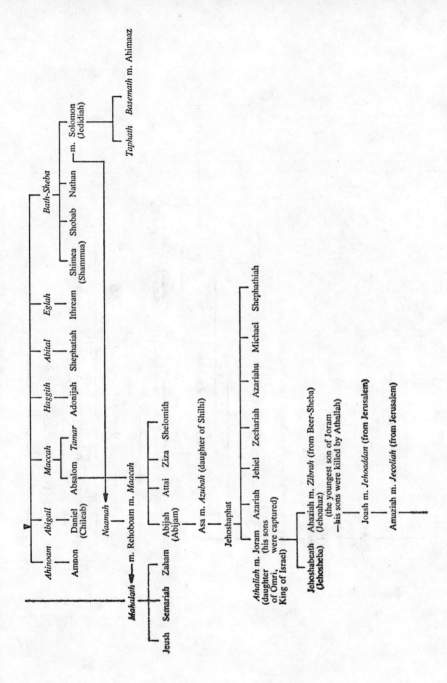

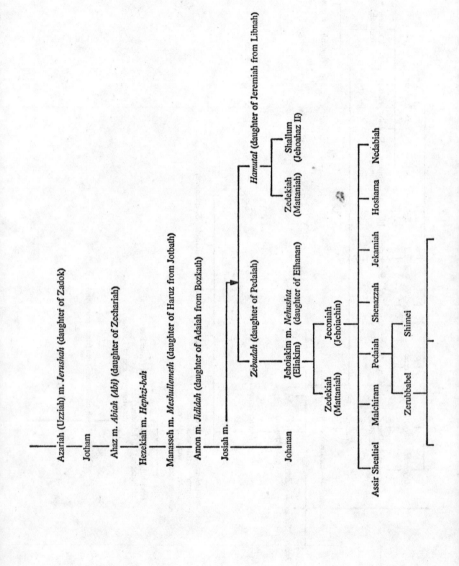

Azariah (Uzziah) m. *Jerushah* (daughter of Zadok)

Jotham

Ahaz m. *Abiah* (*Abi*) (daughter of Zechariah)

Hezekiah m. *Hephzi-bah*

Manasseh m. *Meshullemeth* (daughter of Haruz from Jotbath)

Amon m. *Jidilah* (daughter of Adaiah from Bozkath)

Josiah m.

Zebudah (daughter of Pedaiah)   *Hamutal* (daughter of Jeremiah from Libnah)

Jehoiakim m. *Nehushta* (daughter of Elhanan)   Zedekiah (Mattaniah)   Shallum (Jehoahaz II)

Zedekiah (Mattaniah)   Jeconiah (Jehoiachin)

Johanan

Assir   Shealtiel   Malchiram   Pedaiah   Shenazzah   Jekamiah   Hoshama   Nedabiah

Zerubbabel   Shimei

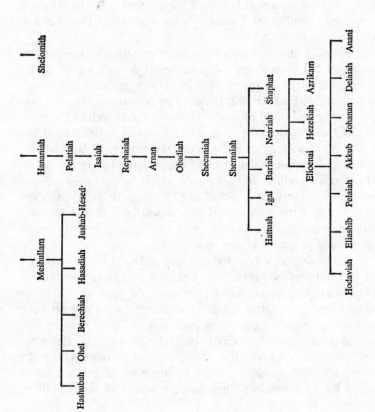

life and the customs of his age. We have been taught that he was a member of the Bethlehemite family of Jesse, a citizen, a leader and authority of Bethlehem, five miles south of Jerusalem. His father, Jesse, is listed in the genealogy of Ruth as the grandson of Boaz and Moabitess Ruth, and thus through his grandparents a descendant of the ancient nobles of Judah. It was Boaz who was a descendant of Nahshon, the son of Amminadab and chieftain of Judah, and thereby a member of one of the most respected families in the tribe of Judah. The story of Ruth reflects Jewish life close to the beginning of the monarchy, about 1000 B.C., and recounts a historical tradition regarding the lineage of the mother of David's family. Ruth left her people, the Moabites, and became a part of Israel, a part of God's chosen people, and therefore God rewarded her. Ruth's son, Obed, was the father of Jesse, and David's grandfather. We know also that David had at least two brothers and sisters.

The family chart on pages 92–95 notes David's genealogy as described in I Samuel and I Chronicles. It describes not only his lineage for forty-two generations but also suggests to our imaginations a brief history of Israel. The successive list of kings sparks at once a rapid review of the towering as well as the modest and the disappointing leaders of Israel and Judah. As applied to David's genealogy, the House of David refers to both his ancestors and his descendants; to his entire noble family. David established a bloodline and a dynasty which for centuries enjoyed power and authority in political and religious affairs. It was a dynasty to which the Jews looked with ardent hope in their nation's darkest hours. It is the genealogy of that dynasty and its ties to the roots of Jesus, which we now explore.

The genealogical table of the House of David is reflected in a list of the kings of Judah from Solomon to Josiah; the sons of Josiah and their descendants (see chart on page 94); the lineage of Jesse through a list of his children (see chart on page 92); and a record of the wives and sons of David born in Hebron and Jerusalem (see charts on pages 92 and 93). Regrettably there is little information in the biblical accounts about the House of David during its reign. In the Book of Kings there is only a list of successive kings and the names of their mothers, while simply the names of the kings of Judah from Solomon to Josiah are recorded in I Chronicles 3:10–14. Also named are the sons of Rehoboam and the sons of Jehoshaphat. The list of Solomon's governors mentions, incidentally, two of Solomon's married daughters, Taphath and Basemath.

The idea that Israel was to be ruled by the descendants of the House of David is first expressed in Nathan's vision (II Samuel 7:16): "And thine house and thy kingdom shall be established for ever before thee; thy throne shall be established for ever." With the continuation of the dynasty's rule over Judah the idea of an eternal royal House of David became firmly rooted, and with the passage of time became the symbol of God's love for his people. Twenty kings, all descendants of David, occupied the throne in Judah for an average of seventeen years each. Even those prophets, who throughout Israel's history sharply and outspokenly opposed the kings of their days, saw in the nation's future the appointed leadership of a descendant of the House of David.

After David's death his descendants reigned over the kingdom of Jerusalem until the Babylonian invasion of 586 B.C. Biblical sources recounting the exile to Babylon and the return to Zion make very little mention of the House of David. For example, the books of Ezra and Nehemiah do not even mention that Zerubbabel was a member of that noble family, although, in Haggai's prophecy he is characterized as the destined ruler of Israel. From the genealogical list in I Chronicles, it appears that Zerubbabel was a grandson of Jehoiachin. It was widely believed that Sheshbazzar, the prince of Judah at the beginning of the Return to Zion, was also of the House of David, and that he is to be identified with Shenazzar, son of Jehoiachin. There are eleven generations of the family recorded after Zerubbabel. If we allot twenty-five years to a generation, there is a documentation of the existence of the House of David until the middle of the third century before the birth of Jesus. However, the glamour and glitter of David's monarchy was greatly dimmed and diminished across the decades by his successors. The people longed for a restoration of national power and purpose which reflected the glory of David's reign.

The rebuilding of the Temple in Jerusalem following the Return to Zion under the leadership of Zerubbabel, about 520 B.C., aroused hope among the people that there would be a renewal of the reign of the Davidic dynasty. The prophecies of Haggai and Zechariah echo that fervent desire. Yet, it is ironic to note that during the period of the Return to Zion the House of David was in eclipse. We are not sure why it was in decline. Zerubbabel or his descendants did return to Babylon; for among those who came with Ezra was Hattush who was related to Zerubbabel. Yet we know nothing of the Davidic family in Babylon and whether or not they lived at court surrounded and supported by royal favors and appointments. Nor is it clear why the family, or at least part of it, returned to Judah with Ezra.

Nonetheless, there is a clue for us to ponder as we consider the fortunes of the Davidic house. After the return of the Jews to Zion from Babylon there was a clash between the descendants of David and the high priesthood of Judah. The controversy ended in victory for the priesthood. The conflict weakened the position of the House of David, undermining the link between them and the future fortunes of Israel. Even during the period of the Second Temple, Judaism did not abandon the ideal of a redeemer from the bloodline and dynasty of David, but this hope now became a telescoped ideal for the distant future and no longer a strong theme and force in contemporary Jewish history.

Details regarding David's descendants after about 400 B.C. are few and incomplete. If descendants existed, they played no prominent role in the political or religious affairs of the people. The nation's disappointment after the excitement of Zerubbabel's days was critical, and expressions of hope for the renewal of the kingdom through the leadership of the House of David disappear. As we turn the pages of the books of Malachi, Daniel and Enoch, there appears a reference to a redeemer who is superhuman, rather than merely a future king of the dynasty of David.

David's reign was a time of military might and political unity; it was an age of religious glory for a people chosen by God. Against this background hope remained among the Jews that the ancient days would return, and the people longed for a ruler "from the stem of Jesse," from among the descendants of David.

The hope for an "anointed one," a Messiah who would rekindle
the flash and sparkle of David's reign, must be viewed through
glasses which see the subsequent decline and humiliation of Israel: the disarray of the monarchy at home, the disgrace of Exile
in Babylon, the religious waywardness of the priests and the
people . . . all encouraging the hope for an age of restoration.
When Judea came under Roman rule (63 B.C.) a wave of oppres-
sion was unleashed by the conquering forces and officials. This
outburst of persecution triggered a religious revival throughout
the countryside, a renewal which was accompanied by the messianic hopes for a redeemer descended from the House of David.

The source of much of the later biblical interest and emphasis
on the Davidic ancestry of the Messiah is anchored in God's
promise to David in II Samuel 7:11-16:

> Also the LORD telleth thee that he will make thee an house.
> And when thy days be fulfilled, and thou shalt sleep with thy
> fathers, I will set up thy seed after thee, which shall proceed out
> of thy bowels, and I will establish his kingdom.
> He shall build an house for my name, and I will establish the
> throne of his kingdom for ever.
> I will be his father, and he shall be my son. If he commit iniq-
> uity, I will chasten him with the rod of men, and with the stripes
> of the children of men:
> But my mercy shall not depart away from him, as I took it
> from Saul, whom I put away before thee.
> And thine house and thy kingdom shall be established for ever
> before thee: thy throne shall be established for ever.

In this Old Testament passage the Davidic king is recognized
as the son of Yahweh and the family line is certain to continue
forever. In the eighth and seventh centuries B.C., the prophets
Amos and Hosea remarked that the future Davidic ruler in Israel, who would renew the ancestral line, would be a redeemer
and not a political leader. The prophet Isaiah comments of "a
shoot from the stump of Jesse, and a branch . . . out of his
roots"; he looks forward to the age of Yahweh's victory over the
forces of evil when "the root of Jesse shall stand as an ensign to
the peoples." The prophet Jeremiah, who warns the house of
David of its collapse because of its waywardness yet underscores

the continuity of the Davidic family line as well as the expectation of a "righteous Branch to spring forth from David," in a
forceful message seems to expect a Davidic renewal: "But (in
that day) they shall serve the Lord their God and David their
king, whom I will raise up for them." And Ezekiel the prophet
declared the new David would be a shepherd who also serves as
prince and king over Israel. Whenever a future "Messiah" is expected in the Old Testament, he is to come from Judah and from
the House of David.

Later Jewish literature also emphasizes the Davidic ancestry
of the Messiah. In the book of Ecclesiasticus 47:22 of the Apocrypha, the endlessness of the House of David is again noted:

> But the Lord will never leave off his mercy, neither shall any
> of his works perish, neither will he abolish the posterity of his
> elect, and the seed of him that loveth him he will not take away:
> wherefore he gave a remnant unto Jacob, and out of him a root
> unto David.

We find the expectation of a Davidic Messiah forcefully expressed in IV Ezra 12:32.

> This is the Messiah whom the Most High has kept until the
> end of days, who will arise from the posterity of David . . .

While the seventeenth chapter of the Psalms of Solomon links
the future Messiah with the Davidic line:

> Thou, O Lord, didst choose David (to be) king over Israel,
> and sweardst to him touching his seed that never should his
> kingdom fail befor Thee (Verse 4).
> Behold, O Lord and raise up unto them their king, the son of
> David, At the time in which Thou seest, O God, that he may
> reign over Israel thy servant (Verse 21).

These last lines were penned by their author about 63 B.C., at the
time when Jerusalem was captured by the Roman General Pompey. The writer was a man with a firm and fixed opinion; he was
strongly opposed to any monarch who was not of the lineage of
the house of David. He speaks sharply and critically of the Mac-
cabee family who had seized the throne of David. Yet he did not
suggest the name of an heir-apparent waiting in the wings to be

anointed king. There is no trace of evidence in the psalmist's verses that he knew of the whereabouts of any descendants of David in his day. At this time, about fifty years before Jesus was born, no family in Israel had any genealogical proof of descent from King David.

Jesus' roots, as recorded in the genealogies in Matthew and Luke, are traced directly to David. He is addressed by people who hear and see him as the "Son of David." As the Gospel accounts were written near the end of the first century after Jesus' death they indicate that there was a strong tradition among Christians that Jesus was of the House of David. Those who believed that Jesus was the Messiah concluded that he must indeed be descended from David.

VII

GENEALOGY OF JESUS:
MESSIANIC EXPECTATIONS

Behold, the days come, saith the LORD, that I will raise unto
David a righteous Branch, and a King shall reign and prosper,
and shall execute judgment and justice in the earth.

In his days Judah shall be saved, and Israel shall dwell safely;
and this is his name whereby he shall be called, THE LORD OUR
RIGHTEOUSNESS.

(Jeremiah 23:5–6)

One of the greatest gifts which the people of Israel have given to
the world is their belief in the Messiah, the Redeemer who is
to come, who will rescue the people of Israel from their suffering in exile and who will lead them home again to Jerusalem. Serious scholars have debated for centuries the origins of
the belief in the Messiah. Some find its roots among the Assyrians while others propose that the Egyptians or Persians or
Babylonians were the founders of messianic belief. Conversely,
the Greeks did not have any real messianic expectations in their
religious practice or customs.

For us to fully comprehend the uniqueness of this gift from
the people of Israel to the world, we must understand the history
of the Jews, their hopes and goals, their achievements and disap-
pointments, their strengths and weaknesses. Throughout their
history Jews have remembered that they were in a special sense
God's chosen people. Because of that distinctive relationship
they naturally expected a very special place in the world. In the
early dawn of their history as a wandering nomadic people they
looked forward to a permanent settlement, a land that they

could call their own, a land of abundance, flowing with "milk
and honey." They were led to the wilderness, across the Red Sea
and into the land of Canaan by their god Yahweh.

The word Messiah has enjoyed several meanings over the
passage of time. Originally, as used in the Bible, it meant
"anointed" and referred to Aaron and his sons, who were anointed
with oil and thereby consecrated as High Priests to the service of
God. The High Priest was called "the Anointed of God." We
should remember that none of the patriarchs—Abraham, Isaac or
Jacob—were "anointed," nor were Moses or Joshua. When the
Philistines threatened to overrun Israel and there was a need for
a strong, courageous and bold leader to direct Israel's army, the
eleventh-century prophet Samuel was moved to anoint first Saul
and then David. With the establishment of the monarchy, the
term "anointed" was applied to the king. He was "the Anointed
of the Lord" because he was installed into his high office by re-
ceiving the sacrament of anointment. Finally, the prophet was
also submitted to the ceremony of anointing. Elijah, for example,
was commanded by God to anoint Elisha as a prophet in his own
place.

During the early days of the monarchy of Israel, say about 970
B.C., the person of "the Anointed of the Lord" came to be considered holy; to hurt him, or even curse him, was a capital offense.
There was also a special belief that God provided protection to
his anointed king. While David was king of Israel the belief developed that his descendants would not only reign over Israel
forever, but also over all nations:

> It is God that avengeth me, and that bringeth down the people
> under me . . .
> Therefore I will give thanks unto thee, O LORD, among hea-
> then, and I will sing praises unto thy name.
> He is the tower of salvation for his king: and sheweth mercy
> to his anointed, unto David, and to his seed for evermore.
>
> (II Samuel 22:48, 50–51)

Thus, the messianic idea was firmly established during David's
kingship: The king in ancient Israel was also the Lord's Messiah.
David, son of Jesse, became for later Jews the model of the Mes-

siah. His days as king were regarded by the Jews as the greatest days of their history. His charismatic political leadership unified all of the tribes of Israel, forging them into one powerful nation. His acts of heroism and courage in battle against Israel's enemies became for his people and successive generations a litany of nationalism and power. In war he crushed Israel's enemies, while in peacetime he was the architect of a mighty nation.

David's spiritual leadership also shaped him in the minds of his people as the ideal kind of King-Messiah. In the Bible we read of David carrying out acts of extraordinary cruelty, but we also read of his confessing his sins and repenting of them. We read of him loving his tirelessly difficult son, Absalom, more than his own life; and of his forgiving Saul, who hated him, with gentle kindness when Saul's life was in his hands. We read still later of his sorrowing over Saul's death and allowing the court prophet Nathan to say whatever was on his mind, while all the time as king vigorously concerning himself with the national religion. David's carefully fashioned political talents supplemented with deep sensitive religious and ethical qualities stamped him as the model of the redeemer and the founder of the ruling family from which the Messiah was to be descended. The name "son of David" became a title for the King-Messiah, and so too was the name David itself.

With the collapse of the Davidic empire following the death of his son Solomon, there arose in the hearts and minds of the people the hope that the House of David would again rule over Israel and Judah, uniting the nation within and protecting it from its neighboring enemies. The Jewish people did not distinguish and separate their spiritual life from their political life: They imagined their Messiah to be at once a spiritual and political leader. For the people of Israel, the Age of the Messiah represents a future Golden Age when hope and prayer will be joined with the coming of the redeemer, the son of David. In contrast, other ancient peoples in the Near East fastened their idea of a Golden Age to past eras.

More than two centuries after David, the Hebrew prophets began to shift their attention from the turbulent present to the promise of the future. The prophets' task was not to talk smoothly to kings and people but to tell them what was right; they were preachers and reprovers; they were the true prophets waging war against the false prophets. The people of Israel had become a nation; they had been redeemed from slavery in Egypt; they had received the law; and they were committed to a life of obedience to God and a religion which ever reminded them of their dependence on God's forgiveness and mercy. Yet, the Israelites were constantly forgetting their relationship with God and their promises to him. Idol worship, civil war, immorality and complacency eroded the tie between God and his people; and the nation needed to be reminded time and again of its purpose. The prophets were men raised up by God to call the people back to God and his way.

The message of the Old Testament prophets belongs to the period of the nation's decline, the Exile of its people to Babylonia and their ultimate return home. Spanning a period from about 800–530 B.C., most of the prophets directed their messages to the rulers and people of the southern kingdom of Judah. The prophets Isaiah, Joel and Micah broadcast their messages during the era prior to the fall of Jerusalem to the Babylonians in 587 B.C.; while Jeremiah, Habakkuk and Zephania were active at the time of the fall of the city and during the Exile; Haggai, Zechariah and Malachi spoke their prophetic words following the return of the Jews to Jerusalem in 538 B.C. and soon thereafter. Of still other prophets we can say they carried out special missions: Hosea and Amos to the northern kingdom, Israel, which fell to the arms of Assyria in 733 B.C.; Jonah and Nahum within the Assyrian capital of Nineveh; Daniel in Babylon; Ezekiel among the Jewish exiles in Babylon; and Obadiah in Edom, Israel's neighbor and long-time enemy.

Here we are concerned with only one aspect of the prophetic messages: their description of the bright future state God has in place for his people in a messianic kingdom. The covenant between Yahweh and King David was recast with new meaning by the prophets Amos, Hosea, Micah and Isaiah. They all spoke of hope and of the coming of a future ideal king who would reign over Israel in the glory of David and lead the nation out of its turbulence and divisions. The prophets' solution for internal social, political, economic and moral distress was the enthronement of a perfect king. A monarch who would establish and lead a perfect society creating peace among all neighbors and nations. The future age is seen as one instituting the perfect covenant relationship. It is an age described as centered around some great coming Person. The new ruler was to be a descendant of David's family line:

> Behold, the days come, saith the Lord, that I will raise unto David a righteous Branch, and a King shall reign and prosper, and shall execute judgment and justice in the earth.
> In his days Judah shall be saved, and Israel shall dwell safely: and this is his name whereby he shall be called, THE LORD OUR RIGHTEOUSNESS.
>
> (Jeremiah 23:5–6)

Isaiah was the prophet with the keenest vision of the ideal David and the perfect future for God's people. His interest, and indeed that of all of the prophets, was not the birth of the future king but rather his accession to the throne of David's house. He wrote:

> Therefore the Lord himself shall give you a sign; Behold, the virgin shall conceive, and bear a son, and shall call his name Immanuel.
>
> (Isaiah 7:14)

This person was to be the mighty God occupying David's throne:

> For unto us a child is born, unto us a son is given: and the government shall be upon his shoulder; and his name shall be called Wonderful, Counsellor, The mighty God, The everlasting Father, The Prince of Peace.
> Of the increase of his government and peace there shall be no end, upon the throne of David, and upon his kingdom, to order it, and to establish it with judgment and with justice from henceforth even for ever. The zeal of the Lord of hosts will perform this.
>
> (Isaiah 9:6–7)

The new ruler according to Isaiah, is to be a suffering servant:

> He is despised and rejected of men, a man of sorrows, and

acquainted with grief: and we hid as it were our faces from him; he was despised, and we esteemed him not.

Surely he hath borne our griefs, and carried our sorrows; yet we did esteem him stricken, smitten of God, and afflicted.

But he was wounded for our transgressions, he was bruised for our iniquities: the chastisement of our peace was upon him; and with his stripes we were healed.

(Isaiah 53:3-5)

Note how the scene has shifted from the joyous announcement of David's heir to a lonely figure who bears the whole burden of sin, separating mortals from God. Eight centuries before Jesus, Isaiah clearly foresaw him. He knew why he must come and what he would do. He foresaw the son of David giving his life for humanity, and he foresaw God raise him high in exultation.

Amidst the Assyrian siege in the eighth century B.C., the prophet Micah denounced the rulers, priests and prophets, deploring their exploitation of the helpless, their dishonesty in business and their mockery of religion. Micah announces that God's judgment will fall on Samaria and Jerusalem, and only after that will there be restoration. Micah sees a glorious future, when Jerusalem becomes the religious center of the world, and Bethlehem gives birth to a greater David who will rule over all of God's people:

But thou, Beth-lehem Ephratah, though thou be little among the thousands of Judah, yet out of thee shall he come forth unto me that is to be ruler in Israel; whose goings forth have been from of old, from everlasting.

(Micah 5:2)

Micah proclaims that in the new messianic era even the Assyrian will be overcome. Judah too will be purified in that day, and all that she relied on in place of God will be destroyed: armies, defenses, witchcraft and false gods.

Among the most frequently read and best-thumbed sections of the Old Testament is the Book of Psalms. The Book of Psalms is really the Old Testament's hymnal, declaring in sharp colorful words the whole range of human feeling and experience. There are psalms which plead with God and psalms which praise him;

appeals for forgiveness, or the slaying of enemies; prayers for the king, or for the nation; psalms which probe life's problems and psalms which boldly celebrate the greatness of God's law. Some of the psalms blend many of these themes, but all of them are part of the religious tradition of Israel.

We want to focus our attention on only one aspect of the Psalms: the expectation of the Messiah. Nowhere in the one hundred and fifty psalms do we find the Messiah mentioned by name, but his presence is foreshadowed as later generations of Jews came to realize. The New Testament writers, as we have seen, were quick to tie these verses to Jesus as the prophesied Messiah.

Messianic expectation is an important element in the "royal psalms," particularly Psalms 2, 21, 72, 89, 110. In these passages we read of an ideal divine king who is also a high priest and supreme judge—characteristics which were never fully realized in any real king of Israel. Only the "coming great Person," the Messiah, combines these three roles in the ageless universal reign of peace and justice imagined by the psalmists. Words and pictures were presented by the psalmists which were not only accurate regarding Jesus' life and suffering, but which the New Testament writers applied to Jesus as the "anointed one." The links are fastened in several instances: Psalm 2 states, "Yet have I set my king upon my holy hill of Zion. I will declare the decree: the LORD hath said unto me, Thou art my Son; this day have I begotten thee" (verses 6–7). This theme of the power and the rule of God is echoed again in the Acts of the Apostles when the author writes: "God hath fulfilled the same unto us their children, in that he hath raised up Jesus again; as it is also written in the second psalm, Thou art my Son, this day I have begotten thee" (Acts 13:33). Psalm 110, a royal poem associated with King David notes in reference to the Messiah: "The LORD hath sworn, and will not repent, Thou art a priest for ever after the order of Melchizedek" (verse 4). The psalmist is speaking of the ideal person, the king and priest, that was realized fully in Jesus as the New Testament writers make plain: "For he testifieth, Thou art a priest for ever after the order of Melchisedec" (Hebrews 7:17).

For more than forty years the prophet Jeremiah warned the

last five kings of Judah of impending disaster and appealed fu-
tilely to the nation to turn back to God. With the death of godly
King Josiah in 609 B.C., political and religious affairs took a sharp
turn for the worse. Judah was sandwiched between two contend-
ing and belligerent world powers: Babylon to the north and
Egypt to the south. It was Babylon which emerged as supreme
among the Near-Eastern nations and became the tool of God's
judgment upon his godless people. In 587 B.C. the army of Nebuchadnezzar of Babylon invaded Jerusalem, sacked the city and
took the people captive into exile. The dreams of the Jews of an
ideal monarch who would reign over Judah were shattered in
the disorder, violence and turbulence which followed the Exile.
The captives seem to have been moved to Babylonia itself, living
in various towns and villages as well as in the capital city. As far
as scholars have learned, they were free to move about and establish themselves as part of the community, to practice their
own traditions and religion as they wanted. Yet the Exile had
profound and lasting effects on Israel. Many Jews became con-
fused and skeptical about their faith and their traditions. Use of
the Hebrew language declined and with it those who cared for
the Torah. The Temple had been destroyed and animal sacrifices
stopped. Jews of the *Diaspora* were tempted to violate the exact-
ing dietary laws and break other religious ceremonial rules. No
longer was it clear what God required from his chosen people.

As the Exile continued, more Jews defected from the faith of
their fathers, succumbing to their captors' demands that they
worship idols. Doubtlessly they were dazzled and impressed by
the splendor of ancient Babylon. Some of the Exiles may have
felt that the god of Babylon, Marduk, was superior to the God of
Israel. Elements of pagan religion began to fill the voids created
by skepticism and doubt. Some Jews dabbled in astrology and
the occult, moving slowly into these areas before Jewish leaders
realized what was happening. In time, Jewish mystics began to
reinterpret the traditional Jewish teachings in light of the pagan
beliefs they had heard and accepted. This created a sharp ten-
sion between Jews who embraced pagan practices and those
who did not, and it caused the Jews to split into several factions
after the Exile. Some Jewish leaders felt that the returning Jews

should renounce their pagan ways, while others believed they should relax some requirements of the Law.

Not all Jews surrendered to pagan beliefs during the Exile. Many Jewish leaders realized that these ideas threatened the survival of the Torah. Without the Law, Jews would have no hope. Religious compromise would lead them farther and farther away from God's Word until they were lost among the neighboring cultures. Responding to this threat, Jewish leaders established synagogues, instituting the office of rabbi and emphasizing the need for a faithful "remnant." These changes guaranteed the survival of Judaism, but also aided the creation of new factions among the Jews.

The empire of the Babylonian kings was not to endure forever. The last king, Nabonidus, saw his nation and people fall to Cyrus, the Persian, in 539 B.C. The Persian monarch's policies were generally peaceable, and he allowed the Jews to return home and restore Jerusalem's Temple. When the exiles returned to Jerusalem there were intense struggles for power and position between the priests and the descendants of David. Political and religious strife and turmoil were common: Where the monarchy was to have flourished, it was weak and ineffective; where there was to be righteousness, there was corruption; where justice was to have reigned, there was unfairness.

The prophet Haggai, who proclaimed his "word from the Lord" in 520 B.C., addressed the governor, Zerubbabel, grandson of Jehoiachem, king of Judah and a descendant of David. Haggai spoke of the new age, the era of the Messiah, reminding Zerubbabel that he was only a representative on earth of Yahweh, the real ruler. In the difficulties of the last days, when the thrones of foreign kings will collapse, the messianic age of salvation will begin and, according to Haggai, Zerubbabel will be the Messiah of Yahweh standing in a close relationship with God. It is to Zerubbabel the heir to David's throne, rather than to Zerubbabel the individual, that these messianic promises are made. He stands in the family line between David and Jesus.

Writing about 520–518 B.C., the prophet Zechariah details many references to the Messiah which are fulfilled in the life of Jesus. He writes of two anointed persons who are at work,

Zerubbabel and Joshua, agents of the community of Yahweh who have the right to stand before him. Zerubbabel is designated the messianic king of the last days which are now dawning. During his reign the countryside will bud and blossom again and the building of the Temple of Yahweh will be completed. Zechariah denotes an important relationship between the Messiah and the high priest; there is to be no more rivalry between the two, the priest is to be subordinate to the Messiah and is to take the place of honor at the right hand.

The prophets of the post-Exile period had no other alternative than to dream away the turmoil, hard times and purposelessness of their day. Malachi, whose name means, incidentally, "my messenger," was active between 460 and 430 B.C. His era was one of disillusionment: The long-promised prosperity was still to come and the people felt that the words of the prophets were false, that God's action in their lives, the lives of his chosen people, was disappointingly incomplete. There was an increasingly casual attitude toward worship and maintaining the standards God had set. Malachi spoke to the people that though corruption among the Levitical priests was now the rule, there would come a day when their ceremonies and offerings "will be pleasant unto the Lord as in the days of old" (Malachi 3:4). Although waywardness and backsliding was now common, Yahweh "will send you Elijah the prophet before the coming of the great and dreadful day of the Lord" (Malachi 4:5). There followed in these decades of uncertainty and disappointment a community without a king, a people ruled by a priestly dictatorship. The priest and not the king was "the anointed one."

Malachi restated the familiar message, the Lord *is* coming, first to purify his people and then to judge them. Looking forward to a new age he proclaimed:

> Behold, I will send my messenger, and he shall prepare the way
> before me: and the Lord, whom ye seek, shall suddenly come to
> his temple, even the messenger of the covenant, whom ye delight
> in; behold, he shall come, saith the Lord of hosts.

> (Malachi 3:1)

With these stirring words of Malachi, Old Testament prophecy falls silent. Four hundred years later, God sent one last prophet, John the Baptist, to announce the coming Messiah. For more than four centuries Palestine remained a pawn in the struggles of succeeding Near-Eastern imperial powers. The might of the Babylonians was followed by the Persians and Greeks. The armies of Alexander the Great captured Palestine from the Persians in 332 B.C. and introduced the divisive cultural influence of Hellenism among the Jews. In every land that he conquered, Alexander the Great promoted Greek culture. In Palestine he required the Jews to adopt the language and customs of Greece, and Jewish scholars began reading Greek philosophy in the libraries of Alexandria and other cities of Alexander's empire. They were dazzled by the ideas of Aristotle and other Greek thinkers, especially when they saw the achievements of Alexander's Greek civilization.

After Alexander's death in 323 B.C. his generals divided his empire. Ptolemy I established a dynasty in Alexandria. His forces attacked and captured Jerusalem, bringing back Jewish captives to colonize the area around his capital city in Egypt. Ptolemy made them full citizens in his new empire and invited Jewish scholars to use the famous libraries of Alexandria. Another of Alexander's generals, Seleucus I, established a dynasty in Syria, and he eventually pushed the Ptolemies out of Palestine. But the Seleucids gradually lost control of the Palestinian frontier until the Seleucid king, Antiochus III, was defeated by the Romans in 190 B.C. The Romans made the Seleucid Empire a satellite of their own growing empire, and because of their own Greek heritage, the Seleucids continued to impose a Greek way of life upon their Jewish subjects.

Following the repressive decrees issued in 168 B.C. by Palestine's Seleucid rulers Antiochus Epiphanes and Antiochus IV, which were aimed at destroying the religion of Israel and replacing it with the worship of Greek gods, dormant messianic interests were revived among the Jews. While the fabric of religious life was being torn apart by political leaders, it was also being undermined by highly placed religious figures and in particular the priesthood. Antiochus IV had to pay heavy tribute to the Roman Emperor, and in order to raise this money he decided to

sell the office of Jewish High Priest. First he gave it to Jason, a
brother of the high priest Onias III. Two years later Jason's
friend Menelaus offered to pay three hundred talents more for
the office, so Antiochus removed Jason and put Menelaus in his
place. After installing Menelaus as high priest, Antiochus went
on a rampage, confiscating the property of Jerusalem's citizens
and ransacking the Temple to fill his treasury. Then he set up a
pagan altar in the temple, where he sacrificed a pig, a violation
of the Mosaic Law. Antiochus ordered his subjects to build
Greek altars in all the villages of Palestine. He outlawed the Mosaic rituals, punishing those who attempted to observe them. Antiochus and the radical Greek leaders demanded, on pain of
death, that all Jews transfer their loyalties from God to gods. For
the Jews, who had been called by God to be his special people,
this was blasphemy. They were forcibly sandwiched between
apostasy on the one hand and an unknown fate on the other.
Loyal Jews searched for a constructive and useful alternative to
their problem.

Four possible solutions took shape: First, the Jews could cling
to God's endless power to save them and they, in turn, would be
prepared to die rather than violate his law. Second, there could
be a revival of prophetic vision. Third, the Jews could unite and
take up weapons in armed rebellion. Fourth and last, there could
emerge a form of Judaism which would shift its focus from
earthly rewards and punishments to heavenly ones.

The insults of Antiochus IV enraged the Jews of Palestine. In
166 B.C. a group of Jewish rebels began a series of attacks on
Antiochus and his successor in hopes of destroying them. Called
the Maccabean War after one of the rebel leaders, Judas Maccabeus, the conflict was waged from 166–143 B.C. The cry was
heard for everyone who was "zealous for the law, and maintained the covenant" to join the struggle. We do not know how
many Jews joined the Maccabeans, but the rebels seemed to
have had popular support.

As the Maccabean War dragged on, the Jewish forces were
able to regain more and more of Palestine. A new treaty was
made with Rome to assure that the Romans would intervene if
the Syrians launched an all-out war against the Jews. At last the

Maccabeans controlled most of the Promised Land, and they named their leader Simon "governor and high priest forever until there should arise a faithful prophet." By doing this they established Simon's family as a new line of priests. Simon's descendants were known as the "House of Hasmon," or Hasmoneans. His third son, John Hyrcanus, named himself king and high priest in 135 B.C., beginning a new Jewish dynasty that would last until the Romans invaded Palestine.

Antiochus IV died in a campaign against the Romans in 128 B.C., and the Jews now had a free hand to govern themselves in Palestine. They revived the sacrificial system established by the Law of Moses, hoping to bring a new golden age to Israel. But the Torah, the written law, was not directly the standard for their new Jewish state. Instead, the people followed oral traditions received from rabbis who had taught their ancestors during the Exile. Over six hundred years Jews of the *Diaspora* had developed many different interpretations of the Law, suited to the situations in which they lived.

During the second century B.C. there was a revival of interest in prophecy. The book of Daniel echoes this interest, and was probably written during the second century B.C. by an author who adopted the name of the sixth-century prophet. Daniel recovered the messianic theme which had blossomed in an earlier day. He spoke of the "Son of Man," of the coming of an "anointed prophet" and held out hope for the resurrection of the dead.

With the growing weakness and corruption of the ruling Hasmonean princes and with the people dissatisfied with their reign, hope for a better monarchy begins to appear in Judaea. Secular politics also underlie the struggle between two of the contesting religious factions, the Pharisees and the Sadducees. The Pharisees strongly urged the observance of the Law. They were the party of the scribes and the master interpreters of the oral traditions of the rabbis, thereby exerting a strong influence over the common people. Because the people trusted them, the Pharisees were chosen for high government positions, including the ruling council, or Sanhedrin. The historian Josephus estimates that only six thousand Pharisees lived in Palestine dur-

ing the time of Jesus, so they needed popular support. The Sadducees, on the other hand, were allied with the aristocracy and
the wealthy more worldly classes. Doubtless both parties were
caught up in self-interest politics. The Pharisees championed precise fulfillment of God's Law and the keeping of the Sabbath.
They laid new emphasis on the doctrine that Israel's salvation as
a nation must not come from weapons and military victories, but
from God.

The Jews were struggling to fashion themselves as a nation
again. Hasmonean rule had brought a secularization of the
kingdom of God for the sake of a harsh and rapacious aristocracy. The nation threw itself on the side of the Pharisees, with
nationalistic fervor and hope that help would come from Yahweh and his deputy, the long-promised king of David's royal
house.

The Pharisees' solution to the problem of Roman persecution
and the grip of Roman procurators was a faith in "the world to
come" and "the resurrection of the dead." Their eyes were on individuals and their eternal life and not on the uncertainties and
unfairness of this world. The community of the Pharisees was
universal; it was not dependent on either the land or the temple
but on its selection by Yahweh. The Pharisees were yearning for
salvation. The arrival of a Messiah, who would free them from
the grasp of the Romans and restore the House of David, would
in their minds only create a problem rather than provide an answer. They were concerned with salvation, with life beyond the
grave, not freedom from pain and suffering or national independence. To the Pharisees, the Romans had a right to take a census
of the population and levy a tax; for the Romans were ruling the
everyday world, while the Pharisees were seeking entrance to
the world to come.

While many Jews embraced the system of the Pharisees, large
numbers were drawn to other alternatives. One of the alternatives was a revolt against Rome and the establishment of a Jewish state. Another was the prospect of the coming of a charismatic leader, a Messiah, who would sweep away the tyranny of
Rome and bring in the kingdom of God as promised by the
prophets. The messianic alternative was uncertain: The pro-

phetic visions were not specific. They did not name names or give dates. They did not declare whether the Son of Man was to be a son of David or whether there was to be a specific person at all. It was against this background of messianic uncertainty that Jesus began his ministry.

As a Jew, Jesus had been taught the doctrines of the Pharisees and had learned their faith in the world to come and their steadfast belief in the resurrection of the dead. He used, too, the Pharisaic style of recalling scripture, drawing freely on any verse which would cast light on a particular situation. Yet Jesus differed from the Pharisees as he based his teaching of the coming kingdom on his own personal authority, as if he were the Son of Man or a prophet like Isaiah or a Son of God or the Messiah. These were the claims which the Pharisees could not accept, and in attempting to refute them they had to develop some idea of the Messiah, since they were faced with scriptural evidence signaling that a Messiah had been foretold by the prophets of the sixth, seventh and eighth centuries before Jesus. It was a notion that while affirming that a Messiah, a son of David, would come, no would-be Messiah, least of all Jesus, could ever meet the necessary conditions. Among these were: first, a genealogical descent from David; second, a public display of signs and wonders; third, the return of Elijah before the Messiah; and fourth, the fulfillment of his messianic mission during his lifetime demonstrated as having been spelled out by the early prophets.

According to the Pharisees, Jesus could not be the Messiah since: He appeared to deny descent from David; he did not perform convincing signs and wonders; it was not agreed that Elijah had appeared prior to Jesus' ministry; and Jesus was crucified, a form of execution for common criminals which appeared to cancel his messianic claims. Nevertheless, the Gospels insisted that Jesus was of Davidic roots, did indeed perform signs and miracles for those who had faith in him, that Elijah had come in the person of John the Baptist and that Jesus fully confirmed that he was the Messiah by his resurrection.

The connection between its Jewish roots and the messianic age of Christianity flows from the belief that God had made a promise to David, his anointed, to establish David's throne forever; to the prophetic connection of an ideal Davidic king with a perfect future; and then to the Pharisaic belief in a world to come and the Resurrection. These ideas found convincing renewal in the crippling experience of the Jews under the Roman procurators, an experience that was ultimately to drive even the most loyal followers of the Pharisees into a suicidal war against Rome. Such turmoil stirred up the memory of the agony which had prompted Amos, Hosea, Isaiah and others to create a perfect solution to such distress: a kingdom of God, and a perfect king.

By the time of Jesus' birth it was clear that the long-hoped for greatness of the Jews was a dream that could never be achieved through natural means. For centuries they knew neither freedom nor independence: The ten tribes were carried off to Assyria and lost forever; the Babylonians conquered Jerusalem and carried the Jews away captive; the Persians came as their masters; then the Greeks and finally the Romans. The great days of David's reign seemed unlikely to return even though the prophets had spoken of a day when there would come another king of David's family line who would make them great in righteousness and in power.

A new dream grew up, anticipating a day when God would intervene in history and achieve by supernatural means that which natural means could never accomplish. They looked for God's power to do what human power was unable to do. During the period between the writings of the Old and New Testaments there were many books written which forecast a new age shaped by God's interest and action. These books were apocalypses, a word which means unveilings, particularly of the future. It is these books which describe to us what the Jews believed in the time of Jesus about the Messiah and the work of the Messiah and the new age. It is in terms of their message that we must see the message of Jesus.

The themes of the books of apocalypses follow similar patterns. Before the Messiah came there would be a period of terrible tribulation; the world would be turned upside down. Honor and decency would be shattered and physical and moral life would become chaotic. There would be "quakings of places, tumult of peoples, schemings of nations, confusion of leaders, disquietude of princes" (4 Ezra 9:3). Into this world of disorder would come Elijah to herald the arrival of the Messiah. He was to mend disagreements and prepare the way for the Messiah. Then the Messiah would enter, a superhuman person bursting into history to remake the world. The Messiah would be the most destructive conqueror in history destroying his enemies. There would be a renewal and purification of the city of Jerusalem, and the Jews who were scattered all over the world would be gathered within the walls of the new city. This new world was to be a Jewish world, a strong element of nationalism was clear at the time. Palestine was to be the center of the world and reign over all nations. The new age would be one of peace and goodness which would last forever.

Consider Jesus undertaking his ministry against a background of messianic ideas which were violent, nationalistic, destructive and vengeful. No wonder he had to teach his disciples the new meaning of Messiahship.

VIII

EARLY CHRISTIAN WRITERS

> The reason that Matthew does not put any but natural sons is
> because he composes the physical genealogy. The reason that
> Luke puts adoptive and legal sons is because he composes the
> spiritual genealogy.
>
> (Albertus Magnus)

EARLY CHRISTIAN WRITERS

For nearly two thousand years scholars and teachers have debated and discussed the genealogies of Jesus as recorded in the
Gospels of Matthew and Luke. The topic has attracted the attention of church historians and theologians from every quarter
within the church, in both the Greek and Latin traditions and
from Antioch to Rome to Canterbury. The study of the roots of
Jesus has fascinated not only orthodox Christian scholars but also
zealous Christian critics. In A.D. 200 attention to Jesus' genealogy
was partly fashioned by church thinkers and leaders in response
to opposition from Jewish religious leaders and from early Christian heretical groups such as the Gnostics.

Early Christian tradition firmly identified Jesus as a descendant of King David, the most noble of royal blood in Israel. It
was not, however, a mantel which Jesus wore easily or lightly,
and he never openly or pointedly claimed that distinction. Mark
reports at one point in his Gospel (12:35–37) that Jesus refuted
the scribe's belief that "Christ is the Son of David"; yet earlier,

Mark (10:47) seems to give approval to the tradition of Jesus' Davidic descent when the blind beggar Bartimaeus of Jericho calls Jesus the "Son of David" and Jesus does not deny the title.

St. Paul, the eloquent preacher and widely traveled evangelist, firmly identified himself in his Epistle to the Romans about A.D. 55 as an apostle of the Gospel "Concerning his Son, Jesus Christ our Lord, who was made of the seed of David according to the flesh" (Romans 1:3). This Pauline tradition is perhaps two or three decades older than the writings of Matthew and Luke. At no other point in Paul's letters to young churches does he refer to Jesus' genealogical link with David.

In hopes of quieting the sharp and persistent criticism and opposition of Jewish leaders the church found it persuasive to show Old Testament prophecies fulfilled in Jesus. One of the most powerful summaries of this kind was made by Justin Martyr (flourished A.D. 138–167), also called Justin the Philosopher. Born in Samaria of pagan parents, he studied philosophy and at about the age of thirty-eight was converted to Christianity at Ephesus. Thereafter he traveled from city to city to convert men of some learning. It was while he operated a school in Rome, teaching Christian philosophy, that he was martyred under Emperor Marcus Aurelius. Of his writings only two remain today, the *Apology* and the *Dialogue*. The *Apology* is a refined, cogent and tutored defense of Christians against charges of atheism and sedition in the Roman state. It also presents an invaluable record of the customs and practices of second-century Christianity. The *Dialogue* is no less important as it sets forth in the form of an argument with the Jew Trypho a reasoned philosophic defense of Christian beliefs, particularly with reference to Jewish writings. Justin's sweeping and magnetic grasp of the Old Testament books discovered within them messianic prophecies which found their fulfillment in Jesus. Moses, first of the prophets, foretold of the Messiah:

> The sceptre shall not depart from Judah, nor a lawgiver from between his feet, until he come for whom it is reserved.

>   (1 *Apology* 32; Genesis 49:10)

And Isaiah, the prophet, spoke thus:

> A star shall rise out of Jacob, and a flower shall spring from the
> root of Jesse, and his arm shall the nations trust.
>
> (1 *Apology* 32; Isaiah 11:1)

Importantly, Justin concluded in his *Apology* that by the power
of God Jesus was conceived by the Virgin Mary who was, according to him, a lineal descendant of Jacob and Judah, the father of the Jews. It is essential to note that this second-century
author identifies Mary and not Joseph as the descendant of the
royal house of David.

The controversy over Jesus' divinity was not limited to its denial by traditional Jewish leadership, but it extended to another
group of critics, the Gnostics, who in turn denied Jesus' humanity and his death. Consequently, in the fast current of second-
century Christian religious thought, we find an appeal to Jesus'
Davidic roots for proof on one hand of his Messiahship and on
the other as proof of his true human nature. We find these
themes stated in the writings of St. Ignatius of Antioch (d.c. A.D.
107). He was the first writer to stress the virgin birth of Jesus
and with his pen firmly denounced the heresy and Docetism
which denied Jesus' humanity, as well as the criticism of Jewish
leadership who denied Jesus' divinity. He wrote to the church at
Ephesus that "There is one physician, composed of flesh and
spirit, generate and ingenerate, God in man, life in death, from
Mary and from God." Further, while Jesus was still fully divine,
being "our God," he was also fully human, a descendant "of the
family of David, and of Mary." Thus, asserted Ignatius, was
Jesus both "the son of Man and the son of God."

From the very beginning Christianity had not been uniform in
practice or belief, and by A.D. 150 the Gnostic varieties of Christianity had become a serious and troublesome rival to the early
church. This movement within second-century Christianity has
been carefully recounted in Elaine Pagel's recent and important
book, *The Gnostic Gospels*. We will only mention at this time
that the Gnostics and Marcionites rejected the belief that Jesus
was the long-expected Davidic Messiah. They attacked the

human "roots" thesis of Jesus and presented other interpretations as to his origins and the origin of creation.

The Christian God was the God of Creation, the God of Abraham, Isaac and Jacob, the God who sent his Son, Jesus, to save mankind. Gnostics, as we now know from the recent discovery of the Gnostic writings at Nag Hammadi in Egypt, saw the matter in another light. For them the God of creation and of the Old Testament was an inferior and evil power. The Gnostics believed that originally there had been only a realm of spiritual being, and that the spiritual being had become fragmented and divine sparks had become trapped in matter for this intention by evil powers. These evil powers attempted to imprison the divine "soul" ensnared in the matter of the body and the created world, by making the soul sleep or exist in a state in which it forgets its spiritual origin. Thus it was necessary for a Redeemer to descend from the spiritual realm to awaken these sparks by imparting the *gnosis*, or knowledge, of the person's true condition and of his spiritual origin.

The Redeemer-Revealer in many Gnostic theological systems is the Christ. However, since matter is evil, this Christ either unites himself with the historical person Jesus, whose body is not of ordinary flesh, or this spiritual Jesus only appears to have a physical body. It was unthinkable and beyond all reason for the Gnostics that the Redeemer could have been of lineal descent from King David as prophesied in the Old Testament. Irenaeus, Bishop of Lyon in Gaul, who was the earliest Father of the Church to systematize Christian doctrine, wrote against the Gnostics while at the same time telling us much about them. He wrote about A.D. 185 that the Gnostic Cerinthus "represented Jesus as having not been born of a virgin, but as being the son of Joseph and Mary according to ordinary human generation . . . After his [Jesus'] baptism, Christ descended upon him in the form of a dove from the Supreme Ruler."

The controversy and conflict with the Gnostics was vitally important for it forced the church's leaders and theologians to describe more systematically and precisely their understanding of Jesus' roots. Irenaeus responded to Gnostic denial that Jesus took descent from the Virgin Mary and thereby any inheritance of the flesh, by declaring:

> Why did he come down into her if he were to take nothing of her? . . . Wherefore Luke points out that the pedigree which traces the generation of our Lord back to Adam contains seventy-two generations, connecting the end with the beginning, and implying that it is he who has summed up in himself all nations dispersed from Adam downwards . . . Wherefore also Luke, commencing the genealogy with the Lord, carried it back to Adam, indicating that it was he who regenerated them into the Gospel of life, and not they him. And thus also it was the knot of Eve's disobedience that was loosed by the obedience of Mary. For what the virgin Eve had bound fast through unbelief, this did the virgin Mary set free through faith.

> (*Against Heresies*, 3.22. 1–4;
> Trans. *Ante-Nicene Fathers*, Vol. 1)

The Bishop of Lyon had not only discussed Jesus' genealogy with these words but also set forward a plan of salvation. He stated that sin was brought into the world by Adam, and it was not undone until the birth and resurrection of Jesus. It was, as Luke records in his lineage, Jesus who contained in himself all his descendants and was thereby able to redeem mankind.

Another treatment of Jesus' genealogy in opposition to the Gnostic's position was advanced by Tertullian (c. A.D. 160–c. 230), the Roman theologian and apologist who became the most formidable defender of the faith in his day. He remarked that:

> Matthew, when tracing down the Lord's descent from Abraham to Mary, says "Jacob begat Joseph the husband of Mary, of whom was born Christ" . . . Since he is the blossom of the stem which sprouts from the roots of Jesse, [and] since the root of Jesse of the family of David, and the stem of the root is Mary descended from David, and the blossom of the stem is Mary's son, who is called Jesus Christ, will not he also be the fruit? . . . For every step in a genealogy is traced from the latest up to the first, so that it is now a well-known fact that the flesh of Christ is inseparable, not merely from Mary, but also from David through Mary, and from Jesse through David.

> (*On the Flesh of Christ*, 20–21,
> Trans., *Ante-Nicene Fathers*, Vol. 3)

Tertullian was answering the Gnostic point of view that Jesus did not assume human flesh of Mary but merely came to earth *through* Mary. To support the position that Jesus was at once God and man, Tertullian presented the idea that the Logos of God had impregnated the virgin Mary, who was the descendant of David, thereby fulfilling the prophecy of the psalmist.

> The Lord hath sworn in truth unto David; he will not turn from it: Of the fruit of thy body will I set upon thy throne.
>
> (Psalm 132:11)

Jesus' genealogy was also challenged by the Ebionites ("The Poor"), a Jewish-Christian sect. The Gnostic Ebionites stated that Jesus was the natural son of Joseph and Mary, interpreting the well-known passage of the prophet Isaiah (7:14) as "Behold, a young woman shall conceive," rather than "Behold, a virgin shall conceive." Irenaeus responds again to this criticism and declares:

> He whom God promised David that he would raise up from the fruit of his belly as an eternal king is the same one who was born of the virgin, herself of the lineage of David. For on this account he promised that the king should be "of the fruit of his belly," . . . which was the appropriate [term] to a virgin conceiving and not "of the fruit of his loins," . . . which was appropriate of a man . . . In this promise, therefore the Scripture excluded all virile influence . . . But besides, if indeed he had been the son of Joseph, he could not, according to Jeremiah, be either king or heir. For Joseph is shown to be the son of Joachim and Jechoniah, as also Matthew sets forth in his pedigree. But Jechoniah, and all his posterity, were disinherited from the kingdom, as Jeremiah declares, "As I live, says the Lord, if Jechoniah the son of Joachim king of Judah had been made the signet of my right hand, I would pluck him thence . . ." (Jeremiah 22, 24–25) . . . And again, "Jechoniah is dishonored as a useless vessel. Earth, hear the word of the Lord." Write this man a disinherited person: for none of his seed, sitting on the throne of David, shall prosper, or be a prince of Judah.
>
> (*Against Heresies* 3:21, 5)

This statement is important for us as we explore the roots of

Jesus. Irenaeus was saying, and he has never been given proper credit, that the Messiah could not come from the line of Jechoniah, King of Judah (c. 597 B.C.), as Jechoniah had been disinherited from the kingdom when he was carried away by Nebuchadnezzar to Babylon and imprisoned. Therefore, as Jechoniah is found as an ancestor, Matthew must trace Jesus' genealogy through Joseph's family line. In the prior passage above, Irenaeus understood Luke's record of Jesus' genealogy as belonging to Mary.

Late in the second century, A.D. about 178, the pagan Roman philosopher Celsus launched a bitter literary attack against the Christians. He was an opponent of Christianity, and while his writings have been lost, the substance of his *True Discourses* was provided some years later by Origen, the most famous of the Alexandrian theologians, in his book, *Against Celsus*. An erudite and profound biblical scholar, Origen was a prodigious author and certainly the most important theologian in the church before St. Augustine. Celsus had charged in *True Discourses* that "the mother of Jesus was turned out by the carpenter who was betrothed to her, since she had been convicted of adultery and had a child by a certain soldier named Panthera." Origen crisply responded to this criticism of Jesus' roots by writing that Celsus:

> Did not mention at all the discrepancy between the genealogies which is a problem discussed even among Christians, and which some bring forward as a charge against them . . . But he [Celsus] says, "the men who compiled the genealogy boldly said that Jesus was descended from the first man and from the kings of the Jews." He thinks he makes a fine point in saying that "the carpenter's wife would not have been ignorant of it had she had such a distinguished ancestry." . . . Why just because she was ignorant of it, should it be untrue that she was descended from the first man (cf. Luke), and that her descent went back to the rulers of the Jews?
>
> (*Against Celsus*, 2:32)

Here again we see that Luke's genealogy was accepted as Mary's lineage.

Celsus was not the only pagan to level a sharp pen in an attack on Christian teachings and beliefs. The Roman Emperor, Julian the Apostate (c. A.D. 331–363), through his studies, embraced pagan ideas and abandoned Christianity. He did not attempt, however, during his reign, to regularly persecute the Christians; in fact, he issued an edict of toleration. But he did try to restore paganism as the religion of the Roman Empire, causing great confusion within Christianity, a church already divided internally over many theological quarrels. Julian did not miss referring to the discrepancies in Matthew's and Luke's genealogies in his own attack on Christianity.

As we consider the replies of Christian authors to the writings of the Jews, Gnostics and pagans, an important theme emerges: The early Christians stressed Jesus' kinship with David through Mary and not through Joseph. To follow the roots of Jesus through Joseph allowed too many opportunities for critics to deny the humanity or divinity of Jesus.

By the late second century the four Gospels of the New Testament were generally accepted, and the Christians began to turn their attention from debating with their non-Christian opponents to controversies among themselves regarding differences in the Gospel texts and methods for interpreting the Scriptures. The tone of the disagreements and debates among Christians over the genealogies is on a different plane than the previous disputes with non-Christians. Christians could accept among themselves that Jesus was somehow both God and man and that the Scripture was true. The discussions began to focus on precisely how Jesus was God and man, and it was as a consequence of these debates that the first systematic analysis was written of the Matthew and Luke genealogies.

THE GREEK CHURCH

In 1969 Professor Marshall Johnson published in his important book, *The Purpose of the Biblical Genealogies,* the translated Greek text of an anonymous manuscript fragment which until that time had not been brought into the discussion of Jesus' genealogy. The fragment reads as follows:

Joseph the husband of Mary, of whom the Christ was born, descended from the Levitical tribe, as the divine evangelists showed. But, on the one hand, Matthew brings down from David through Solomon to Joseph, and, on the other hand, Luke through Nathan, but both Solomon and Nathan were sons of David. Both the evangelists passed over in silence the birth of the holy virgin, since it was not the Hebrew custom nor of the divine Scripture to give the genealogies of women, but it was the law that members of one tribe were not to be betrothed to those of another tribe. Joseph certainly descended from the Davidic tribe took as spouse the holy virgin, since she was from the same stock—showing that they were satisfied with the stock of Joseph. It was the law that if a man died childless, his brother married the widow, and raised seed for the deceased; indeed the child, according to nature, belonged to the second who had begotten [it], but by law [he belonged] to the deceased. Therefore, from the lineage of Nathan, the son of David, Levi, begot Melchi; and from the lineage of Solomon, Matthan begot Jacob; and when Matthan died, Melchi, the son of Levi, who was of the tribe of Nathan, married the mother of Jacob, and begot by her Heli. Therefore, Jacob and Heli were uterine brothers—Jacob being of the tribe of Solomon, and Heli from the tribe of Nathan. Then Heli from the tribe of Nathan died childless, and Jacob took his brother's wife, and he begot Joseph, and raised up seed for his brother. Therefore, Joseph is the son of Jacob by nature, descending from Solomon, but by law [the son] of Heli [descending] from Nathan."

(Marshall D. Johnson, *The Purpose of the Biblical Genealogies*, Cambridge, 1969, pp. 273–75)

These genealogical relationships may be viewed on the following chart.

Thus, the anonymous fragment claimed both a Levitical, priestly and Davidic royal descent for Joseph. Similarly, Irenaeus in his book *Against Heresies* stated that Luke's list of ancestors illustrated his "priestly character," while Matthew's records showed his human nature. The Christian historian Sextus Julius Africanus disputed earlier theories which suggested that the mixing of both priestly and royal men in Jesus' genealogy was made to show Jesus as both priest and king. Africanus' solution which ap-

Chart on Levirate Marriage of Joseph's Parents According to Anonymous Manuscript Fragment

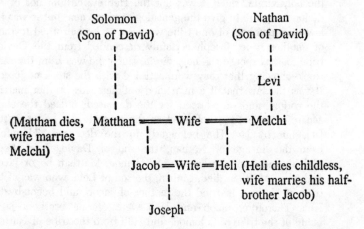

Matthew's Royal/Human Genealogy   *Luke's Priestly/Spiritual Genealogy*

Solomon   Nathan
(Son of David)   (Son of David)

Levi

(Matthan dies,   Matthan ═══ Wife ═══ Melchi
wife marries
Melchi)

Jacob ═ Wife ═ Heli   (Heli dies childless,
                       wife marries his half-
                       brother Jacob)
Joseph

(Son by Nature)   (Son by Law)

peared about A.D. 220 in his *Epistle to Aristides* essentially agrees with that advanced by the unknown author of the Greek fragment. Both writers explain the genealogical differences by a form of marriage known as Levirate (from the Latin word *levir*, meaning husband's brother). The differences in the genealogical record were explained on the grounds that Matthew had recorded Jesus' physical ancestors while Luke noted his legal forebears.

Examples of Levirate marriages are found in the stories of Judah and Tamar in Genesis and in the question the Sadducees put to Jesus:

> Moses said, If a man die, having no children, his brother shall marry his wife, and raise up seed unto his brother.

(Matthew 22:24)

The law as stated in Deuteronomy reads:

> If brethren dwell together, and one of them die, and have no
> child, the wife of the dead shall not marry without unto a
> stranger; her husband's brother shall go in unto her, and take her
> to him to wife, and perform the duty of an husband's brother
> unto her.
>
> And it shall be, that the firstborn which she beareth shall suc-
> ceed in the name of the brother which is dead, that his name be
> not put out of Israel.
>
> (Deuteronomy 25:5–10)

This law would apply only to Jacob and Heli who were related,
and not to Matthan and Melchi who had no direct family ties.

To close our discussion of Julius Africanus and the anonymous
Greek manuscript, it is essential to recognize that the Levirate
marriage solution came to dominate the interpretations of Jesus'
roots until the Reformation. So, too, did the insistence that both
the genealogies of Luke and Matthew traced Joseph's lines. Despite Africanus' forceful objections, many church leaders continued to explain the differences between Matthew's and Luke's
records by human-divine or priestly-kingly solutions or a pro-
phetic-royal interpretation. The latter position was based on the
confusion of Nathan the son of King David with Nathan the
prophet, who were not at all the same person.

From the third to sixth centuries the church was engaged in
an intense debate regarding the nature of Jesus. The debate was
focused on distinguished Christian theologians and teachers in
two communities: Antioch and Alexandria. The scholars at Antioch looked at the New Testament Scriptures with an eye for the
literal, not the hidden sense of the author; at Alexandria, the authors were primarily concerned with the eternal and spiritual
truths found in biblical texts and not with historical facts. The
tendency of the Antiochenes was to emphasize the humanity of
Jesus while the Alexandrians focused on his divine nature.

The Alexandrian theologian who cast the longest shadow not
only during his lifetime but throughout the Middle Ages was the
aforementioned Origen (c. A.D. 185–254). Like scholars today,
Origen acknowledged that Matthew and Luke had theological

reasons for compiling Jesus' genealogy, and their motives were responsible for the discrepancies between the two records. For Origen the signals to the author's theological motives are found in the structure of the genealogies. Matthew traces the lineage from Jesus' birth through such sinners as Tamar, Rahab, "Uriah's wife," David, Solomon and Rehoboam. Luke begins his genealogy of Jesus after his baptism in the Jordan River by John the Baptist and traces the family line through the prophet Nathan by whom David's sins were rebuked. Matthew's Jesus is he who has come into the world as the Redeemer of sinners; Luke presents Jesus as the descendant of an unblemished line and as the one who purifies his sins through baptism. It is by this method of interpretation that Origen attempts to harmonize the differences between Matthew and Luke's genealogies.

The "Father of Church History," Eusebius of Caesarea (c. A.D. 260–340) in his still valuable *Ecclesiastical History* referred to Africanus' *Epistle to Aristides* and its attempt to harmonize the two genealogies of Jesus. He also concludes, perhaps out of a sense of necessity, by reciting Mary's Davidic lineage:

> And the lineage of Joseph being thus traced, Mary also is virtually shown to be the same tribe with him, since, according to the law of Moses, intermarriages between the different tribes were not permitted. For the command is to marry one of the same family and lineage, so that the inheritance may not pass from tribe to tribe.
>
> (*Ecclesiastical History*, 1.7.1)

Mary's genealogy must be clearly stated, for if it is not, Jesus is dependent upon Joseph's family line for his Davidic inheritance, and that tie would cast reservations on the concept of virgin birth.

Other leaders of the Greek church were concerned too with the significance of Jesus' roots. One of those was Gregory of Nazianzus (A.D. 329–389), a Cappodocian theologian, Doctor of the Church and one of the Four Fathers of the Greek church. A remarkable preacher, theologian and writer, Gregory in one of his poems, *On Christ's Genealogy*, accommodated the differences between Matthew's and Luke's accounts. He declared that from

David were born two sons, Solomon and Nathan, the first being of royal blood while the second had priestly connections. "Christ, however, was of both, the great King and Priest," as illustrated by the two Gospel records. He had to explain how Joseph could have had two fathers, and he does so by discussing the Levirate marriage solution in a manner similar to Julius Africanus. Gregory states that Matthew's list gave Joseph's natural ancestors while Luke recorded his legal line. The question arises, however, as to how Jesus descends from David and Joseph if he was born of the virgin Mary, who was a Levite. It is explained by Gregory that there had been a blending of the royal and priestly tribes during Aaron's time and the Babylonian captivity. The journey to Bethlehem by Mary and Joseph proves, said Gregory, that they were of the same tribe, indicating that Jesus was of the royal blood on his mother's as well as his father's line.

The greatest Father of the Greek church, John Chrysostom (c. A.D. 347–407), was born in Antioch. He studied the Greek classics and began his ministry in that city. His preaching earned him not only wide recognition but also his name, Chrysostom, which means in Greek the "Golden Mouth." In A.D. 398 he was appointed Patriarch of Constantinople where his eloquence, ascetic style of life and charity brought him the admiration of the people. He wrote brilliant homilies, interpreting the Scriptures literally and historically rather than in an allegorical fashion, which gives us a welcome glimpse of fourth-century church life.

In a series of *Homilies on the Gospel According to St. Matthew,* Chrysostom remarked that the genealogy of Joseph is traced, although Joseph was not the father of Jesus, noting that it was not the law among Jews to record the genealogy of women. Matthew, he believed, kept the custom and passed over Mary's lineage in silence listing only Joseph's. Another reason, he declared, was that God did not wish it to be known to the Jews that Jesus was born of a virgin; for if it had been discovered, they would have condemned and stoned her for adultery. He raised the question as to how Jesus' Davidic line can be known when Mary's ancestors were not recorded. John's reply was, "Listen to God, telling Gabriel to go to a virgin betrothed to a

man, of the house and lineage of David. What would you want
plainer than this, when you have heard that the Virgin was of
the house and lineage of David. There was a law which made it
unlawful to take a wife from any other stock but from the same
tribe."

Chrysostom spoke too of the four women who appear on
Matthew's genealogical record noting that they earned fame for
the wrong reasons: one was a harlot, another an adulteress, one
of an unlawful marriage while the last one was of a different
race. He interpreted these persons as examples of God's tender
care and power. It was for this cause that Jesus came, not to escape our disgraces, but to bear them away . . . and furthermore,
he pointed out, all are under sin, even our forefathers themselves.

The powerful influence and theological authority of the
church leaders of Antioch through the first four centuries was
diminished and finally destroyed when Nestorius (d. A.D. 451?),
patriarch of Constantinople, was condemned for his theological
views at the Council of Ephesus in A.D. 431. He outraged ecclesiastical leaders by opposing the use of the title Mother of God for
the Virgin on the grounds that while the Father begat Jesus as
God, Mary bore him as a man. The Council at Ephesus and
twenty years later at Chalcedon clarified orthodox doctrine pro-
nouncing Jesus as true God and true man, two distinct natures
joined in one person.

Nestorius' friend, Theodoret, bishop of Cyrus in Syria, stood by
his associate and attempted to clarify misunderstandings at the
councils of Ephesus and Chalcedon regarding Nestorius' theological positions. He too was a theologian of considerable ability
and wrote on a variety of historical, moral and theological topics.
In his volume *Questions and Answers to the Orthodox* he refutes
the pagans' argument that Jesus' title "Son of Man" indicated
that he was born of physical intercourse, claiming that if Jesus
had been born of such a manner, the Bible would not have said,
"who was supposed to be the son of Joseph."

If Joseph was regarded as Heli's son according to the law,
rather than from intercourse, and if God gave Joseph to Heli as a

son in this fashion, why should it be surprising that he also gave Joseph a son without intercourse? Divine Providence ordained that the Virgin would be engaged to a man who had two fathers, one according to nature from conjugal union, the other according to law without conjugal union. "If he who was born from the wife of Heli is Heli's son according to God's law, he who was born according to God's decree is ever more so the son of Joseph without conjugal intercourse" (*Questions and Answers to the Orthodox,* p. 66).

Before we leave our discussion of the Eastern church's interpretations of Jesus' genealogy we should mention the writings of John of Damascus (c. A.D. 675–749). He spent his life largely in fighting with his pen for orthodoxy. His influence was powerful not only in his history of the heresies which plagued the church but also in his stimulation of art and music. He presented in his influential book *On the Orthodox Faith,* a clear statement that Mary was of the house of David. Recalling that Joseph's lineage is set forth in Matthew and Luke as it was not the custom to record the genealogies of women, he also cites the law of a Levirate marriage.

> Born then of the line of Nathan, the son of David, Levi begot Melchi and Panther: Panther begot Barpanther, so called. This Barpanther begot Joachim: Joachim begot the holy Mother of God. And of the line of Solomon, the son of David, Nathan had a wife of whom he begot Jacob. Now on the death of Nathan, Melchi, of the tribe of Nathan, the son of Levi and brother of Panther, married the wife of Nathan, Jacob's mother, of whom he begot Heli. Therefore Jacob and Heli became brothers on the mother's side, Jacob being of the tribe of Solomon and Heli of the tribe of Nathan. Then Heli of the tribe of Nathan died childless, and Jacob his brother, of the tribe of Solomon, took his wife and raised up seed to his brother and begot Joseph. Joseph, therefore, is by nature the son of Jacob, of the line of Solomon, but by law he is the son of Heli, of the line of Nathan. Joachim then took to wife that revered and praiseworthy woman, Anna . . . This Anna, but supplication and promise from God, bore the Mother of God.

With these additional facts concerning Mary, then, the genealogies are reconciled in the following fashion:

Chart on Levirate Marriage of Joseph's Parents According to John of Damascus

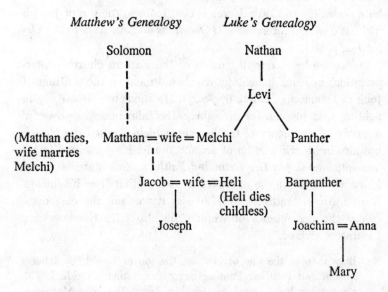

Matthew's Genealogy   *Luke's Genealogy*

Solomon   Nathan

Levi

(Matthan dies,   Matthan = wife = Melchi   Panther
wife marries
Melchi)

Jacob = wife = Heli   Barpanther
          (Heli dies
          childless)

Joseph   Joachim = Anna

Mary

Doubtlessly John of Damascus' work, *On the Orthodox Faith* is the most systematic account of the Greek Fathers not only on Mary but also on key Christian Doctrines. The concern to bring Mary into the genealogy of Jesus as illustrated in the chart above was intended to show the truth of Jesus' virgin birth and his descent from David.

THE ROMAN CHURCH

In the Latin or Western tradition of the church distinguished theologians also discussed and commented on Jesus' roots. The first one to do so was Hilary, Bishop of Poitiers (c. A.D. 315–367?). A convert from paganism, he was a Doctor of the

Latin church. He too remarked that the differences in the New Testament genealogies were because Matthew traced the royal line of succession while Luke noted Jesus' priestly origins. Hilary noted that the two records meet with Salathiel and Zerubbabel and that both lists are correct since the two tribes have intermarried. Jesus, the eternal king and priest, is therefore king and priest by his family links. He found nothing unusual in Matthew and Luke recording Jesus' roots through Joseph rather than Mary since they were both of the same tribe, and all members of a tribe would have been closely related.

Following in Hilary's footsteps was Ambrose (c. A.D. 340-397), the popular Bishop of Milan. An expert theologian, he was advisor to Emperor Gratian whom he persuaded to outlaw all heresy in the Western church. Like John Chrysostom, Ambrose was an eloquent preacher, whose words spurred the conversion of Augustine to Christianity. In his book, *Exposition on the Gospel According to Luke,* Ambrose's treatment of Jesus' genealogies was much the same as the other writings we have discussed. His design was to solve some of the inconsistencies presented by the genealogical records, using as his reference work Eusebius' *Questions to Stephan.* He declares that while the genealogies are of Joseph's line, Mary had to have been from his tribe, as Joseph was a just man and would not have violated the law which required that a man marry within his own tribe. Furthermore, the Annunciation to Mary indicates that she was of David's tribe. He clearly points out that Zacharias and Elizabeth were also from the tribe of Judah. The chief difference in the two New Testament genealogies is the same interpretation we have met before: Matthew gives Jesus' kingly lines whereas Luke records his priestly ties. This still leaves the problem of how Joseph could have had two fathers, and like others before him Ambrose uses Julius Africanus' Levirate marriage solution. However, Africanus says that Jacob raised up seed (Joseph) for his brother Heli while Ambrose has it the other way around, making Joseph the legal son of Jacob, and by nature the son of Heli.

Recognized as the greatest biblical scholar of the early church, Jerome (c. A.D. 347-420?) was also a Father of the Latin church. Educated in Rome in classical studies, he was baptized in A.D.

Chart on Levirate Marriage of Joseph's Parents
According to St. Ambrose of Milan

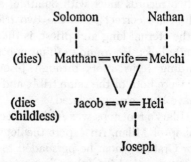

366. Traveling to Antioch to continue his studies, he experienced a vision of Jesus in which he was reproved for his pagan studies. He fled to the desert to live as an ascetic and hermit studying the Scriptures. From A.D. 386 until his death he lived at a monastery in Bethlehem where he did a major portion of his Latin translations of the Bible, known as the Vulgate. It became the standard Bible of the West.

Jerome's treatment of the genealogies is found in the first book of his *Commentary of the Gospel of Matthew* (A.D. 389). This is a bit of writing which he wrote in a hurry, within two weeks, for a friend who had requested reading material for a sea voyage. He was not concerned with the differences within the texts of the Gospels, but his work, nonetheless, became the standard reference source for Medieval scholars.

As to why Joseph is said by Matthew and Luke to have had different fathers, Jerome recounts the Mosaic law of Levirate marriage to his friend, remarking that one was the legal father while the other was the natural one. Like a modern scholar adding a footnote or two to his text, Jerome refers his friend to the writings of Julius Africanus and Eusebius of Caesarea who analyze and comment on the problem at greater length.

Why did the genealogists list Joseph, when he "was not truly the father of the Lord of Salvation"? "First," Jerome noted, "it was not the custom of the Scriptures that the line be composed by generations of women. Second, Joseph and Mary were from the same tribe, from which he was compelled to take her as wife, and because together (with her) he was taxed at Bethlehem it is clearly seen that they were from the same stock."

Another towering figure in the West was Augustine (A.D. 354–430), one of the four Latin Fathers. Raised as a Christian, he rejected the faith of his youth, living a wild and dissolute life in Carthage. At some time in his youth he was a convert to Manichaeism, which was a radical Gnostic religion that absorbed elements of Zoroastrianism, Buddhism and Jewish-Christianity. According to this system, there were two co-eternal principals of Light (good) and Darkness (evil): The King of Darkness became envious of the Light and waged war against the Light, capturing some of its particles. In order to imprison these particles, the King of Darkness created Adam and Eve, whose bodies were of a devilish substance, and whose carnal lust and physical procreation were the devices of the Devil, for it was by these means that the particles of Light were held captive by the Darkness. Therefore, Jesus is sent forth from the Realm of Light as a Savior to the captured particles of Light.

In A.D. 384, at the urging of the Manichaeins, Augustine left Rome, where he taught rhetoric with great success, and moved to Milan to teach. These years were critical ones in his life as he now questioned the doctrines of Manichaeism. Troubled in mind and spirit he fell under the influence of Ambrose, Bishop of Milan. After two years of mental doubt he embraced Christianity and was baptized on Easter, A.D. 387. Soon afterward he returned to his hometown, Tagaste, where he lived with friends in a monastery. While visiting Hippo in North Africa in A.D. 391 he was chosen, against his will, to be priest of the Christians there and remained in that city the rest of his life.

Augustine's influence on Christianity is thought by many learned scholars and teachers to be second only to that of St. Paul. Theologians, both Roman Catholic and Protestant, look upon him as the founder of theology. His earliest discussion of the New Testament genealogies was in a work written in opposition to the Manichaein leader, Faustus, "who in blasphemous fashion, was attacking the Law and Prophets, and their Lord,

and the Incarnation of Christ, and who was also saying that the
writings of the New Testament, by which one refutes them [the
Manichaeins], are false." As a Manichaein, Faustus naturally
rejected Christ's human nature, and he rejected the proof of
Christ's human descent as found in Matthew and Luke because
the Gospel authors disagreed with one another. Augustine therefore set out to refute Faustus by reconciling the genealogies.

We need to keep in mind as we consider Augustine's discussions of the genealogical records the chronology of the writings
in which he examined such matters: *Against Faustus* (A.D. 397);
Gospel Questions (A.D. 397); *On the Harmony of the Evangelists*
(A.D. 400); Sermon 1 (c. A.D. 400–420); *Questions of the Hepta-
teuch* (A.D. 419); and *Retractions* (A.D. 426–427). It is necessary
to do this since Augustine's treatment of the topic changed over
the years, and toward the end of his life he published the *Retractions*, in which he surveyed and corrected his earlier writings. His style was to raise questions about the biblical text and
then provide an answer. We will review his questions one at a
time, and only the most significant ones, as Augustine's writings
on the subject were extensive.

Augustine reconciled the differences in the records of
Matthew and Luke by suggesting that Joseph may have had two
fathers. However, he did not appeal to the Levirate marriage solutions in his early book *Against Faustus*, but rather developed a
more familiar concept in the Roman world, that is to say, adoption. Later, perhaps after holding in his hands a copy of Julius
Africanus' *Epistle to Aristides*, he retracted his adoption solution and inserted in its place the Levirate marriage solution.

Augustine also confronted the question as to why the genealogies are traced through Joseph and not Mary. Certainly, earlier
church leaders and theologians had been troubled also by the al-
legations that Jesus was the natural son of Joseph and that, if he
was indeed born of the Virgin, he might not be of Davidic lineage. But let him speak for himself:

> But seeing that the Apostle Paul unmistakably tells us that
> "Christ was the seed of David according to the flesh," how much
> more ought we to accept without any hesitation the position that

Mary herself also was descended in some way, according to the laws of blood, from the lineage of David?

(*Harmony of the Evangelists,* 2:1–2)

Another matter which has captured the attention of scholars over the last fifteen hundred years is Matthew's numbering of the generations. Augustine remarked that Matthew lists fourteen generations from Abraham to David, fourteen from the era of David to the Exile into Babylon, and from the Exile to the birth of Jesus another fourteen generations are noted. He remembers too that Luke recorded seventy-seven generations in his genealogy of Jesus, and in both instances he declares that the use of numbers is meant to express the remission and abolition of all sins. Since Jesus himself had no sin, there was no sin carried in his flesh linked to the sinfulness of his ancestors. Augustine continued:

This perfect removal of sins the Lord himself also clearly represented under the mystery of this number, when he said that the person sinning ought to be forgiven not only seven times, but even unto seventy times seven. A careful inquiry will make it plain that it is not without some reason that this latter number is made to refer to the purging of all sins. For the number ten is shown to be, as one may say, the number of justice in the instance of the ten precepts of the law. Moreover, sin is the transgression of the law. And the transgression of the number ten is expressed suitably in the number eleven . . . Thus, too, inasmuch as all time in its revolution runs in spaces of days designated by the number seven, we find that when the number eleven is multiplied by the number seven, we are brought with all due propriety to the number seventy-seven as the sign of sin in its totality.

So, then, seven times eleven, that is, as has been explained, the transgression of righteousness, which has regard only to the sinner himself, make up the number seventy-seven, in which it is signified, that all sins which are remitted in Baptism are contained. And hence it is that Luke ascends up through seventy-seven generations unto God, as showing that man is reconciled to God by the abolition of all sin.

(Sermon 1:35)

An important variation in Julius Africanus' solution to the problem of Joseph's two fathers was proposed by "The Venerable Bede" (c. A.D. 673–735), an illustrious English monk. A Benedictine, he spent his whole life at the monasteries of Wearmouth, at Sunderland and Jarrow, which is today within the boundaries of the city of Durham. A biblical scholar and historian he is often referred to as "the Father of English History." In the late seventh and early eighth centuries he was perhaps the most learned man in Western Europe, and his writings comprised a compendium of knowledge for his time covering such wide-ranging subjects as theology, history and science. Like a modern university scholar, he read many documents, discussing their relative merits and reliability and acknowledging them as sources . . . an unusual practice for his time. He wrote biographical works, such as the lives of St. Cuthbert and the *History of the Abbots* (of Wearmouth and Jarrow). His *Ecclesiastical History of the English Nation* written in Latin, remains an indispensable account of English history between A.D. 597 and 731. It provides the most thorough and reliable account of the triumph of Christianity as well as the growth of Anglo-Saxon culture in Britain.

In his writings on various books of the Bible, Bede was dependent on the works of those authors who preceded him: Ambrose, Jerome, Augustine and Gregory the Great. His treatise, *A Brief Exposition on the Gospel of Luke,* leans on Julius Africanus' writings to solve the problem of Joseph's two fathers, but with one notable change. Bede observed that Africanus listed Melchi as Joseph's grandfather in Luke's record whereas the received text for the Gospel identified Matthat as that family member. Interestingly, many early church theologians and leaders, such as Gregory of Nazianzus, Ambrose and Augustine, seemed to have accepted Africanus' solution without ever noticing this discrepancy. However, the Venerable Bede in noting this discrepancy inferred that perhaps Matthat had two names: Melchi and Matthat. So, Bede proceeded to insert Matthat's name for that of Melchi's in the text of Africanus, producing the following modification:

Chart on Levirate Marriage of Joseph's Parents According to the Venerable Bede

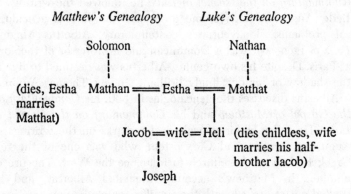

Matthew's Genealogy   Luke's Genealogy

Solomon   Nathan

(dies, Estha Matthan ══ Estha ══ Matthat
marries
Matthat)

Jacob══wife══Heli (dies childless, wife
                              marries his half-
                              brother Jacob)

Joseph

This change of name thereafter became traditional in all subsequent texts of Luke's list of the roots of Jesus.

During the period between the ninth and twelfth centuries, centuries frequently referred to by historians as the "Middle Ages," there was a serious decline in learning throughout Europe. Yet it was a period during which the Christian church became a unifying force. Indeed, even as early as the collapse of Rome in 476 Christianity had become the standard-bearer and instrument of Western civilization. The Papacy gained secular authority and established monasteries throughout Europe. It was from these monasteries that missionaries were sent to convert the Germans, the Angles and the other tribes. Throughout this era little was written on the subject of Jesus' genealogy.

There were no novel contributions by theologians to an understanding of Jesus' roots during the eleventh and twelfth centuries. Anselm (c. A.D. 1033–1109), Archbishop of Canterbury is marked by his many writings as the founder of scholasticism, and his distinguished theological work *Cur Deus Homo* ("Why God Became Man") remains of permanent interest. He taught the immaculate conception of Mary in *De Conceptu Virginali,* and his treatment of the Matthew and Luke genealogies in *Homily 8* is very much the familiar and traditional interpretation.

The Franciscan scholastic theologian Bonaventura (c. A.D. 1217–74), who taught at the University of Paris with Thomas Aquinas, recited the common opinion of Jesus' roots. In his *Commentary on the Gospel of Luke* he followed the writings of Bede, Augustine and Jerome to resolve the various genealogical problems. Bonaventura's contemporary, Albertus Magnus (c. A.D. 1200–80), was a Dominican and a professor of theology at Paris. Despite his own genius, Albertus was destined to live in the shadow of his dazzlingly brilliant student Thomas Aquinas.

Albertus discusses the genealogies in both his *Commentary on the Gospel of Matthew* and his *Commentary on the Gospel of Luke*. He relies in his genealogical remarks on the writings of Augustine, Jerome and Chrysostom, who was one of the few Greek Fathers of the church to influence the West. The use of numbers in Matthew's account fascinated Albertus, and he spelled out at great length the significance of the numbers fourteen, forty and seventy-seven. Albertus further observes that Matthew's genealogy uses the word "begot" while Luke employs the phrase "who was." The reason for this variation, according to Albertus, was that Matthew placed only natural sons in the lineage, while Luke puts adoptive and legal sons into the record as well. He concludes:

> The reason that Matthew does not put any but natural sons is because he composes the physical genealogy. The reason that Luke puts adoptive and legal sons is because he composes the spiritual genealogy.
>
> (*Commentary on the Gospel of Luke*, 3:28–38)

The high-water mark of the age of scholasticism was the appearance of Thomas Aquinas' *Summa Theologica*. Though incomplete, it was the greatest of the Medieval theological systemizations and is still today the foundation for Roman Catholic theology. Aquinas examines the biblical genealogies in his work, *Commentary on the Gospel of Matthew* and the *Summa Theologica*. He puts forward five hypotheses to resolve the difference between Matthew and Luke's records. First, as Luke presents the view that because of the sins of the Kings of Judah, the Messiah descended from Nathan's family line rather than Solomon's; second, Matthew's genealogy presents Jesus' natural lineage while Luke's, the divine or symbolic line of ascent through a series of virtuous men; third, adoption; fourth, the principle of a Levirate marriage; and fifth, that Heli may have been a relative other than the father. From his words it is clear that Aquinas favors the Levirate marriage solution but does not rigidly advance such an opinion.

Aquinas devotes a section of *Summa Theologica* to the question, "Whether Christ's Genealogy is Suitably Traced by the Evangelists?" He reviews the genealogical problems which had concerned writers for nine hundred or a thousand years, building his position on the works of Julius Africanus and Augustine. His opinions regarding the several differences in the genealogical records are traditional, and he writes at length on the problem as to who was Joseph's father—Jacob or Heli. As the other writers before him, Aquinas embraces the position of the Levirate marriage law.

Thomas Aquinas also focuses on the numerological structure of the New Testament genealogical accounts. Matthew noted that he has enumerated forty-two generations but actually listed forty-one while Luke lists seventy-seven, he writes:

> Again, the number forty pertains to the time of our present life, because of the four parts of the world in which we pass this mortal life under the rule of Christ. And forty is the product of four multiplied by ten, while ten is the sum of numbers from one to four. The number ten may also refer to the Decalogue; and the number four to the present life; or again to the four Gospels, according to which Christ reigns in us. And thus Matthew, putting forward the royal personality of Christ, enumerates forty persons not counting him. But this is to be taken on the supposition that it be the same Jeconiah at the end of the second, and at the commencement of the third series of fourteen, as Augustine understands it. According to him this was done in order to signify that under Jeconiah there was a certain defection to strange nations during the Babylonian captivity; which also foreshadowed the fact that Christ would pass from the Jews to the Gentiles.
>
> (*Summa Theologica*, Part 3, Question 3, Article 3)

In summation, while Aquinas did not introduce any new information relating to Jesus' lineage, he did usefully present a systematic summary of various themes and problems which many writers had addressed since the second century. The compelling questions which were studied and interpreted by the theologians and scholars in Antioch one thousand years earlier were still engaging the mind of the greatest figure of scholasticism in Paris of the late thirteenth century.

IX

REFORMERS AND REFORMATION

> I regard it a wasted effort to want to collate all the names against one another, because we do not have the record. Indeed also it was not written especially for us Gentiles, but for the Jews, who knew it well. It is sufficient that we compare the same so far as we are able. . . . I intend to place the entire relationship according to my conception or my understanding. The one who does it better has my thanks!
>
> (Martin Luther)

It was the men of the Renaissance who first called the period which preceded their own "The Middle Ages." For them this was an era without distinction, a label for centuries of ignorance, barbarism and darkness, separating the end of the classical age from the revival of classical learning. The eleventh and twelfth centuries were decades of vigor and unity. It was a period where links of power and conflict were forged between heads of state and the heads of the church. It was also a period which witnessed the rise of the papacy under the leadership of Gregory VII. He and his successors led the church to prominence and power at the expense of national rulers as well as the emperor of the Holy Roman Empire.

The twelfth century witnessed not only the rise of towns and an exploding growth of commerce but also the first of several crusades to the Holy Land. Before the crusades the Holy Land was known to the Christians of the West merely as a place of pilgrimage. The Holy Land had come under the control of the nomadic Seljuk Turks, and Pope Urban II sounded the call in

1095 for Christendom to go to war for the Holy Sepulchre, promising that the journey would count as a full penance and that the
homes of those absent would be protected by a truce. The battle
cry of the Christians was—God wills it! Echoed by many wandering preachers, the movement spread throughout Europe and
Scandinavia.

The first "crusaders" to reach Asia were peasant bands
brought together by the French preacher, Peter the Hermit, and
the French knight, Walter the Penniless. Lacking discipline and
clear objectives, frightful massacres against Jews were committed by the "crusaders" *en route* to the Holy Land. The peasant
forces began to gather at Constantinople at the end of the year
1096. By the autumn of 1097 these armies had reached Antioch,
which fell the next year after a long siege. On July 15, 1099 the
Holy City was successfully stormed. With their hands still
bloody from massacre in the streets, the crusaders gave thanks
for their victory that very night in the Church of the Holy Sepulchre. A Latin Kingdom of Jerusalem was established and a
Latin patriarch elected. The first crusade was a success, and a
movement had been set in motion which fused Christian and
military ideals. During the period between 1147 and 1272 eight
more crusades were undertaken, but none enjoyed the success of
that first adventure.

Another dynamic element of the twelfth- and thirteenth-cen-
tury church was the founding of the mendicant monastic orders.
In 1210 Saint Francis of Assisi founded the Franciscan order,
while in 1216 Saint Dominic received permission from Pope
Honorius III to establish the Dominican order. Both orders were
influential in expanding the church's interests. The Franciscan
friars wandered about preaching the Gospel and working to pay
for their simple daily needs. They traveled not only within Italy
but also to France, Spain and the Holy Land. Meanwhile, Dominic founded an order which trained a body of educated
preachers, dedicated to holy living, in direct response to the popular criticism that the clergy was poorly educated and that their
manner of living was less than modest. Dominicans became
prominent in the life and teaching of the medieval universities, a
new and rising institution of the thirteenth century.

During this era there seems to have been much less interest among theologians and church leaders, in either the Greek or Roman traditions, on the subject of Jesus' genealogy. Perhaps the scholars of this period believed that all necessary details regarding Jesus' roots had already been exhaustively considered by earlier writers. The changing rhythms and intellectual climate in both the sacred and secular world were also placing higher priority on problems other than Jesus' lineage.

The three centuries following the meeting of the Fourth Lateran Council in 1215 were filled with controversy, conflict, schism and change. That Council was the high-water mark of unity within Christendom, and was the twelfth ecumenical council of the Roman Catholic church. Summoned at the Lateran Palace in Rome by Pope Innocent III, its accomplishments not only sum up the pope's ideas for the church, but also crown the work of his pontificate. However, the luster of the Council's achievement was short lived. The papacy's role in the world of secular politics had already been challenged and undermined by the rising power of the Holy Roman Emperor. The ill-fated crusades of the thirteenth century forever dimmed Latin control of the Mediterranean world. The rise of national communities, particularly in France and England, underscored the shift of power from the universal political authority of the papacy to the authority and rights of secular rulers and their national states. During the fourteenth and the fifteenth centuries the welfare of the individual Christian states began to matter more than the welfare of Christendom taken as a whole, as the struggle between England and France in the Hundred Years War so clearly illustrates. There was upheaval within the church, as well; when the Hundred Years War broke out, the Pope and his court were no longer at Rome but at Avignon, in the south of France. Six popes governed from Avignon before Gregory XI in 1376 returned the Holy See to Rome. There followed a Great Schism upon Gregory's death in 1378 when cardinals convened in both Italy and France to elect his successor. The schism was destined to last more than thirty years scarring and bruising the fabric and influence of the church, and further strengthening the hold of the secular rulers over the clergy within their countries.

While the unity and power of medieval Christendom was dissipated amid secular politics and ecclesiastical controversy, the lead in discussing the roots of Jesus passed over to the early and later reforming leaders of the church. One such ruler was John Huss (c. 1369–1415), the Czech religious reformer. Influenced by the Oxford theologian and philosopher John Wyclif, he also attacked the abuses of the clergy. Huss's concern with the genealogy of Jesus was fully focused on Mary's ancestry. In a sermon entitled, *On the Nativity of the Virgin Mary,* Huss comments on the theological significance of the Virgin's birth and its importance in the birth of Jesus. He remarked particularly on the fact that Mary's name follows the names of three sinful women, Tamar, Ruth and Uriah. Jesus' genealogy indicated for Huss that "Christ, coming for the sake of sinners and being born from sinners took without differentiation the sins of both sexes, achieving this himself, and restored the reputation of females." (Magistri Johannis Huss, *Opera Omnia,* xiii, Prague, 1975, pp. 398–99.)

Huss was the first commentator to declare in writing the humanness of Jesus' ancestors, a family line marked by famous persons and low and shameful figures. He seemed especially drawn to the wayward judges, kings and priests and may have shone his spotlight on those personages to serve his design to point out the ineffectiveness, corruption and abuses among church leadership of his day.

The later Continental church reformers, Ulrich Zwingli (1484–1531), John Calvin (1509–64) and Martin Luther (1483–1546), had little to say about Jesus' roots. They were all drawn to loftier theological issues, such as: the doctrines of Jesus' atonement and resurrection, or the nature of Holy Communion, or the various sacraments of the Church.

Zwingli was a Swiss Protestant reformer, who had received a thorough classical education from his teachers in Basel, Bern and Vienna. He also was influenced by the humanist precepts of the eminent Dutch classicist and New Testament scholar, Erasmus. Unlike Luther, Zwingli became a religious reformer through his studies and not through a personal religious crisis. His independent study of the Scriptures led him to question the teachings of the Roman Catholic Church, and when he became vicar of the

Gross-Munster of Zurich in 1518, he found the democratic institutions of the community receptive to his beliefs. In 1519, he successfully opposed the sale of indulgences in the city, and soon
was preaching against clerical celibacy, monasticism and many
other Church practices. The real beginning of the Reformation
in Switzerland was Zwingli's lectures on the New Testament in
1519. Armed with Erasmus' 1516 edition of the Greek text, he
discarded the writings of Church theologians during the previous five hundred years or more, and proclaimed the sole authority of the Word of God as revealed in Scriptures. Thus, Zwingli's
energies and interests were targeted to theological issues and not
to genealogical difficulties.

Another Swiss theologian, and a more towering figure than
Zwingli in reforming and intellectual circles, was John Calvin.
Born at Noyon, Picardy, he studied the classics and Hebrew at
the University of Paris. He came under the influence of humanist
teaching, rebelled against conservative theology and experienced
a "sudden conversion" in about 1533 and turned all his attention
and his acute intellectual talents to the cause of the Reformation.
As a persecuted Protestant in an age of controversy and conflict,
he found it necessary to have his bags packed and traveled from
place to place seeking refuge. It was during these peregrinations
that he began the task of systematizing Protestant thought in his
most distinguished theological work, *Institutes of the Christian
Religion*. Completed in 1536 and later revised and supplemented, the work contained the essential Calvinist theology. In
the *Institutes* Calvin turned from Catholic doctrine by rejecting
papal authority and accepting justification by faith alone; but
many of his other positions, including the doctrine of predes-
tination, had been foreshadowed by Catholic reformers as well
as the Protestant thought of Martin Luther.

Calvin wrote at length in his *Commentary on a Harmony of
the Evangelists* on the genealogical accounts of Jesus in Matthew
and Luke's Gospels. He addressed and analyzed the two genealogies to determine whether Matthew traces Joseph's ancestry,
while Luke traces Mary's lineage. He concluded that the Gospel
authors did not speak of events known in their day. Calvin
pointed out that it seems unbelievable that this poor and scorned

couple belonged to the house of David, that royal line from
which the Redeemer was to descend. He noted: "If any one
inquires whether or not the genealogy traced by Matthew and
Luke proves clearly and beyond controversy that Mary was descended from the family of David, I own that it cannot be inferred with certainty . . ." The reformer believed that it was the
design of Matthew and Luke to overcome the theological obsta-
cle that both Joseph and Mary were unknown, rebuffed and poor
and gave not the slightest indication of royalty. He rejected the
opinion that Luke's genealogy recorded Mary's line of descent,
declaring it to be Joseph's ancestry.

Despite variations Calvin observed that the two Gospel genealogies agreed substantially with each other but have four key
points of difference. First, that Luke's record begins with Jesus
and ascends to Adam, while Matthew does not carry his account
beyond the holy and elect race of Abraham. Calvin believed that
this arrangement was accomplished for a good reason: God had
chosen for himself the family of Abraham, from which the Redeemer of the world would be born, and as the promise of salvation had been confined to that family until the coming of Jesus,
Matthew does not exceed the boundaries which God had set.
Matthew presents Jesus as belonging to that race of God's chosen people. In Matthew's record we must recall the covenant of
God, wherein he adopted the descendants of Abraham as his
people, separating them from the rest of the nations of the
world. Luke, however, directed his view to a higher and broader
point: Though a Redeemer was promised to Abraham's descendants, we know that ever since the sin of Adam every man
needed a Redeemer. Such a Redeemer was accordingly appointed for the whole world. For Calvin it was the purpose of
God that Luke present Jesus to us as the son of Adam while
Matthew limit him to within the family of Abraham.

The third difference between the genealogies which Calvin
noted was that immediately after David, Matthew puts Solomon
and Luke puts Nathan, indicating that they follow different
lines. Many interpreters have commented on this contradiction
and suggested that Matthew, departing from the natural lineage,
offers the legal genealogy. However, Calvin remarked that it was

more correct to say that Matthew had presented the "legal order" in his genealogy: "Because by naming Solomon immediately after David, he attends not to the persons from whom in a regular line, according to the flesh, Christ derived his birth, but to the manner in which he was descended from Solomon and other kings, so as to be their lawful successor, in whose hand God would establish the throne of his kingdom for ever" (John Calvin, *Commentary on a Harmony of the Evangelists*, p. 86).

Calvin found no inconsistency in the purpose which guided Luke to trace Jesus' roots from Nathan. He noted that it may be said that Jesus cannot be acknowledged as the promised Messiah if he is not a descendant of Solomon. However, he hastily added that though Jesus was not naturally descended from Solomon, he was recognized as Solomon's son by legal succession because he was descended from kings.

The fourth and final point of difference between the two Gospel genealogical records is the diversity of names. From David to Joseph, with the exception of Shealtiel and Zerubbabel, none of the names are identical in the two accounts. Calvin remarked that the reason frequently offered was that the difference arose from the custom among the Jews to have two names. Yet, he was not comfortable with that opinion, as it was impossible to know the method Matthew followed to arrange his lineage of Jesus; although he was more certain that after the Babylonian Exile the same persons are recorded under different names.

The additional number of persons listed in Luke's genealogy, as compared to those recorded in Matthew, was not unusual, in Calvin's opinion, since the number of persons in the natural line of descent is usually greater than the legal line. He speculated that Matthew chose to divide Jesus' genealogy into three sections and to make each part contain fourteen persons, although Matthew actually listed only forty-one generations. According to Calvin, Matthew thereby was free to pass by some names, which Luke could not properly omit, not having restricted himself by that rule. Matthew omitted three kings in his list, and Calvin offered the opinion that this was done because Matthew wanted to confine the three sections of his genealogy to fourteen kings and gave himself little concern in making the choice, as he had a

reasonable lineage down to the close of the kingdom to place before the eyes of his readers. As to the problem that only thirteen
kings appeared on the list, Calvin suggests that this probably
arose from the oversights and errors of the transcribers.

The third key figure of the German Protestant Reformation,
Martin Luther was also a critic of the spirited laxness which
gripped high Church officials and protested the abuse of indulgences, an abuse which had also been condemned by Catholic
theologians but which for reasons of financial gain had not been
stopped by Church officials. His review of the genealogies of
Matthew and Luke are as systematic and thorough as his statements on justification by faith or the nature of the Eucharist.

On September 8, 1522, Luther preached a sermon for the
Feast of Nativity of the Blessed Virgin Mary on the topic of
Matthew's genealogy. Luther was interested in his sermon to
explore and determine whether or not Matthew's and Luke's lists
of Jesus' ancestors identify Mary, as well as Joseph, as a descendant of David. He stated that Matthew traced the line of Jews
through Solomon, while Luke listed his brother Nathan: two
lines, yet from the same lineage, namely from two brothers.
Thus, both genealogies remain in the house of David. With the
grandfather of Joseph their accounts meet: at Matthan, or as
Luke calls him, Matthat. Luther further observed, Mary and
Joseph must be not only from the tribe of Judah and from the
house of David, but from a particular house, that of Matthat,
Joseph's grandfather, because the Messiah must come from that
house. As the Messiah is in Matthat's house, Luther declared that
Jesus' mother also is certainly within it because she was a virgin
and is said to have given birth to the Messiah from the house of
Matthat, David and Abraham.

Luther analyzed the descendants of the house of Matthat and
concluded that Matthat had one son from whom Jesus descended, and it is Heli. He had two daughters named Mary, the
eldest was the mother of Jacob while the younger one was Jesus'
mother. She is a first cousin to Joseph and both are grandchildren, according to Luther, of the same grandfather, Matthat.
Accordingly, he determined that Mary and Joseph are of the
same tribe and ancestry because they are grandchildren of the

same grandfather, children of two brothers, and cannot be closer to one another, unless they are consanguineous brother and sister. Nevertheless, the inconsistencies in the genealogical accounts of Matthew and Luke prompted Luther to state: "I regard it a wasted effort to want to collate all the names against one another, because we do not have the record. Indeed also it was not written especially for us Gentiles, but for the Jews who knew it well. It is sufficient that we compare the same so far as we are able. . . . I intend to place the entire relationship according to my conception or my understanding. The one who does it better has my thanks!"

The voices of other Reformation leaders are silent on the topic of Jesus' ancestry. In England, Thomas Cranmer (1489–1556), ambassador from Henry VIII to the papal court on matters relating to his marriages, as well as Archbishop of Canterbury, did not mention it in the preparation of an English liturgy for use in parish churches promoting the reading of the Bible in English. Upon the accession of the Catholic Queen Mary in 1553, Cranmer was tried for treason, convicted of heresy, stripped of his preferments and condemned to burn at the stake.

To the north, in Scotland, the religious reformer John Knox (1505–72), founder of Scottish Presbyterianism, does not seem to have given any attention to Jesus' genealogy. While in exile on the Continent during the reign of Mary I in 1554, he settled in Geneva and served as pastor of the English congregation. While there he conferred with John Calvin, whom he later consulted on questions of Church doctrine and civil authority. Through frequent letters Knox exerted considerable influence among Protestants in England and Scotland. He fought to remove from power the Catholic regent, Mary Guise, and worked for the adoption of a confession of faith by the estates which abolished the authority of the pope, condemning all creeds and practices of the old Church. Single-minded and strong-willed, Knox was an outstanding Reformation leader, but he was not a commentator on Jesus' ancestry.

The Reformation was a time of turbulence not only within the Church but also within the nation states. Theological debate rang out from the pulpit, both Catholic and Protestant, and echoed throughout Europe. A century and a half of religious wars began with a South German peasant uprising in 1524. Radical religious sects sprung up everywhere: democratic, pacifist, millennarian. They were suppressed violently. Civil war began in France in 1562 between Huguenots, Protestant nobles and merchants, and the Catholic populace, ending in 1598 with the Edict of Nantes tolerating the Protestants . . . an Act which later, in 1685, was revoked in blood. Later Hapsburg attempts to restore Catholicism in Germany were resisted by twenty-five years of fighting. The Peace of Augsburg in 1555 guaranteed religious independence to local princes and cities but was confirmed only after the Thirty Years War, which raged between 1618 and 1648, devastating much of Germany.

The Catholic Reformation, a sixteenth-century movement more popularly known as the Counter-Reformation, arose to meet the Protestant challenge. Although sharing the Protestant contempt for the corrupt practices in the Church, there was none of the image-breaking and tradition-shattering that characterized Protestantism. The Catholic Reformation was led by conservative forces whose goal was to secure the traditions of the Church against the innovation of Protestant theology and against the more liberalizing effects of the Renaissance. The central feature of the Catholic Reformation was the Council of Trent, the nineteenth ecumenical council of the Roman Catholic Church (1545–47; 1551–52; 1562–63), which was convened by Pope Paul III. Its work was to define official theology and correct abuses within the Church, and the subject of Jesus' genealogy never arose during the council.

The Reformation era also witnessed the expansion of Old World interests and religion to the shores of the New World. It was an age of exploration, discovery, expansion and settlement in Mexico, Peru and elsewhere stimulating the European economy with new trade in gold and silver.

Following the Reformation, Christendom entered a new age. The Peace of Westphalia in 1648 ended a generation of war and a century of religious division. During the next century and a half the peace of Europe was often interrupted; but religion was seldom a contributing cause. Yet, the Church's authority continued to be challenged at every turn and its independence curtailed. Kings interfered in Church affairs, confiscated Church wealth, and modified the structure of Church life. In Roman Catholic countries the links with Rome were deliberately loosened, and the movement toward national churches made considerable progress.

During the period between 1648 and 1800 the Church was also the subject of an intellectual challenge. Leaders of the Enlightenment, such as Voltaire and Rousseau, questioned the Church's traditional authority. The role of reason was magnified while that of revelation and faith was reduced. The biblical Scripture was rigorously and often unsympathetically reviewed. Miracles were challenged and prophecy was reconsidered. Christian thought faced a mighty challenge which threatened to strip it of all its uniqueness and authority. The Renaissance, Reformation and Age of Reason carried Christendom over the threshold of the modern world, revealing to them the shortcomings of the old ideas of humanity and the universe, and furnishing them with the essentials for a new perspective. Scholastic orthodoxy was no longer a sufficient instrument for thought or life.

It was against this background that the Doctrine of the Immaculate Conception was pronounced and defined by Pope Pius IX on December 8, 1854. For nearly one thousand years Christians in the East and West revered and worshipped the belief that Mary was free from sin. It was not merely a consequence of mid-nineteenth-century Church interest, but one which had a long history of devotion in the worship of the Church. The tenet was defined as "of faith" by Pius IX in the following terms:

> The doctrine which holds that the Blessed Virgin Mary from the first instant of her conception, was, by a most singular grace and privilege of Almighty God, in view of the merits of Jesus Christ, the Redeemer of the human race, preserved from all stain of Original Sin, is a doctrine revealed by God, and therefore to be firmly and steadfastly believed by all of the faithful.

Roman Catholic thinking held the opinion that the person is truly conceived when the soul is created and infused into the body. Therefore, Mary was exempt from original sin at the first moment of her animation, and grace was given to her before sin could have taken effect in her soul.

We must note that no proof of this dogma can be brought to our attention from the Bible. The first biblical passage which contains the promise of the redemption also mentions the Mother of the Redeemer. The sentence against the first parents, Adam and Eve, was accompanied by the earliest Gospel, which put animosity between serpent and woman; "And I will put enmity between thee and the woman, and between thy seed and her seed; it shall bruise thy head and thou shalt bruise his heel" (Genesis 3:15). The conquerer from the seed of the woman, who should crush the serpent's head, is Christ, the woman at enmity between her and Satan in the same manner and measure, as there is enmity between Christ and the seed of the serpent. The greeting of the angel Gabriel, "Hail, thou that art highly Favoured, the Lord is with thee: blessed art thou among women" (Luke 1:28), indicates an abundant grace and a godlike soul which finds its explanation in the Immaculate Conception of Mary.

In the writings of the early church fathers, in both the Eastern and Western traditions, two key points are recited again and again: first Mary's absolute purity, and second her standing as the second Eve. The fathers call Mary "the tabernacle exempt from defilement and corruption"; "worthy of God, immaculate of the immaculate, most complete sanctity, perfect justice, neither deceived by the persuasion of the serpent, nor infected with his poisonous breathings"; "incorrupt, a virgin immune through grace from every stain of sin"; "a dwelling fit for Christ, not because of her habit of body, but because of original grace"; "a virgin innocent, without spot, void of culpability, holy in body and soul, a lily springing from among thorns, untaught in the ills of Eve. . . . nor was there any communion in her of light with darkness, and when not yet born, she was consecrated to God."

St. Augustine, in refuting the heretical opinions of Pelagius, declares that all the just have truly known of sin, "except the Holy Virgin Mary, of whom, for the honor of the Lord, I will have no question whatever where sin is concerned."

The Church has celebrated for centuries feasts acknowledging the conceptions of John the Baptist (September 23); Mary (December 8), and Jesus (March 25). The Feast of the Conception of Mary became in the course of the centuries the Feast of the Immaculate Conception as the theology evolved regarding the preservation of Mary from all sin, although as late as 1854, the year of the pronouncement of all doctrine of the Immaculate Conception, the feast was known throughout Latin Christendom as the Feast of the Conception of Mary.

Since the mid-nineteenth century, a number of German, French, English and American scholars from time to time have reviewed the biblical genealogies of Jesus. Interest in Jesus' roots does not diminish after nearly two thousand years. On the contrary, in this age of science and nuclear weaponry and of anxiety-ridden peoples, there is renewed interest in the life of Jesus. His influence on the development of the Western mind, spirit and institutions remains profound and pervasive as we seek to understand our own humanity and divinity.

X

SUMMARY AND CONCLUSIONS

> You hold the firmest convictions about our Lord; believing Him to be truly of David's line in His manhood, yet Son of God by the divine will and power; truly born of a Virgin; baptized by John for His fulfilling of all righteousness; and in the days of Pontius Pilate and Herod the Tetrarch truly pierced by nails in His human flesh (a Fruit imparting life to us from His most blessed Passion), as that by His resurrection He might set up a beacon for all time to call together His saints and believers, whether Jews or Gentiles, in the one body of His Church.
>
> (*The Epistle of Ignatius of Antioch to the Smyrnaeans*, Verse 1)

Across the centuries we have set out to review the genealogy, the roots, of a remarkable man, perhaps the most remarkable man who has ever lived. It has been our purpose to attempt to understand the use of genealogy in the context of Jesus' day, not only among the Jews but also among the peoples of the nations surrounding them: nations and peoples who at times marched against the Jews, dividing and conquering them.

Our key sources for studying the roots of Jesus have been the Gospels of Matthew, Luke, Mark and John. The authors of these Gospels remembered oral traditions regarding Jesus' family tree and each encompassed different and distinctive traditions cast in a manner to serve particular religious, political and theological purposes.

We have searched the writings and New Testament commentaries of the early church fathers, in both the Latin and Greek traditions. We have also reviewed the works of key theologians through the past twenty centuries, including such writers as St. Jerome, St. Augustine, St. Anselm, St. Thomas Aquinas and Martin Luther. For more than a thousand years the subject of Jesus' genealogy was of legitimate and critical concern to church scholars. For them that aspect of his life was no less important than his wonder-working miracles or his trial, crucifixion and resurrection.

The *Roots of Jesus* has been written largely from a historian's point of view. Biblical evidence has been searched and researched: commentators on Jesus' genealogy, writing in Latin, French, German or English, have been consulted. No historian will ever know completely the full genealogy of Jesus any more than a historian will understand and trace in detail Jesus' resurrection.

The study of genealogy is of worldwide interest, without distinction as to race, religion or national boundaries. It is found among all people, all nations and all periods of history. The earliest form for transmitting genealogical information was oral, using the memory to recall lists of ancestral names. The numerous and very long genealogies which appear in the Old Testament began as oral accounts and were later written down; yet, they concern only great persons, the fathers of the Hebrew people. A central purpose of these biblical genealogies is to show descent from Adam, Noah and Abraham, although we should note that by the time these pedigrees had become a part of the Jewish Scriptures the idea of racial purity for God's chosen people had already encouraged the keeping of family records.

Nearly everywhere in the ancient world—Egypt, Babylonia, Greece and Rome—the kings and heroes whose lineages were recalled by the poets had their origins linked to the gods, or to persons, such as Romulus, who were regarded as having become divine. Doubtlessly the myths and genealogies of gods and demigods of fanciful and real heroes recounted for ancient peoples the stories of the creation of the world, the first inhabitants, acts of heroic courage and legends of human flaws and weaknesses. Not only were they the means for interpreting and understanding the riddles of life for the inquiring mind, but also for remembering a people's story, a nation's history.

Like their Near-Eastern neighbors, the Israelites kept genealogical lists tracing the ancestry of either an individual or clan or tribe. As tribal and patriarchal traditions were strong in ancient Israel, it was important to maintain the genealogical account of an individual. Pure Israeli descent was essential religiously, tracing the individual back in time through the male line to a historical or mythical personage of the long-lost past. For the individual, descent from a tribe or clan meant that he was descended naturally or by adoption from a common ancestry. Thus, each member of a tribe or clan was able to identify Jacob, the father of all of the tribes of Israel, as his progenitor.

The genealogical lists in the early books of the Old Testament, Genesis, Exodus, Leviticus, Numbers, Deuteronomy I and II, Chronicles, Ezra and Nehemiah recount not only the lineages of the fathers of Israel but also tell the story of God's chosen people. The epical accounts of the creation of the world and of man and woman, the Exile in Egypt, and the building of the Temple in Jerusalem, all dramatically link God and humanity, the Suprahuman with the human in a binding and unique relationship.

The four New Testament Gospel accounts provide us with the clues of who Jesus' contemporaries thought he was. Matthew's genealogy of Jesus ties him to the monarchs and ruling houses of the Hebrews and the Kingdom of Judah. It is the lineage of royalty: Son of Man, Son of God. Jesus, a descendant of the family of David, is acknowledged as the long-expected Messiah, the "anointed one," the heir of David and son of Abraham. Masterful and majestic in detail, Matthew's story of Jesus' roots is not dimmed by its inconsistencies and conflicting details. The lineage records Jesus' ancestry from Abraham through the regime of David, from the rule of Solomon to the downfall of the Kingdom of Judah and from the Babylonian exile to Jesus' birth in Bethlehem. For Matthew, Jesus was the royal Messiah, descended from kings.

Unlike Matthew's record, Luke notes Jesus' roots to David to Abraham through Adam to God, showing the reader and the world that Jesus is the Son of God. Luke and Matthew agree on

Jesus' descent from King David. Jesus was an heir not only of
David's royal line but also tied to the accomplishments and traditions of David's monarchy and the House of David. Luke's
long genealogy of Jesus not only describes his lineage, but provides us an outline of the history of Israel and indicates that
there was not only a divine plan for Israel and the Israelites but
also for Jesus. Luke's genealogy brings Jesus into association with
all humanity and ultimately to God himself.

Mark and John did not recount Jesus' lineage in their Gospels.
Perhaps they felt there was no need to since their audience was
already familiar with Jesus' family history. Mark's Gospel, while
not a biography of Jesus, provides us with a history by the use of
stories—stories which help us to understand the ministry and life
of Jesus from his baptism at the hands of his cousin, John the
Baptist, in the River Jordan to his final journey to Jerusalem
where he entered the city on the back of a donkey. Mark presented Jesus as a Servant of the Lord whose miracles and
wonder-working powers mark him as the Son of God. Yet, Mark
also describes Jesus in a human way, as a man who can be tired,
angry, irritated and troubled. He is at once both human and divine.

John's Gospel is primarily theological and mystical in character. John did not intend to write a biography, and there is no discussion of Jesus' roots. The words of the Fourth Gospel regarding Jesus' origins are at once complex, philosophical and
theological in design, yet eloquently stated in the opening verses
of the book:

> In the beginning was the Word, and the Word was with God,
> and the Word was God.

John's understanding of Jesus as the Logos, the Word made
flesh, stands apart from the genealogical accounts of other New
Testament writers. Blending Greek and Hebrew philosophical
uses of the term "Word," John develops the theme that the
Logos connects God and humanity in this world, the supernatural and the natural, the divine and human. The Word represents the reason of God and, therefore, the reason of the universe, and the Word of God has been made known to us through

the birth, life and death of Jesus. The God who created the heavens and the earth also created a man, who having once lived with God, now lives among men. The Word or Logos began at the beginning: It is the creator and giver of life, and became man in Jesus. As the Son of God reveals the father, so does the Word made flesh reveal the unseen God.

During the first three or four hundred years following the death and resurrection of Jesus, early church preachers and theologians persistently addressed the subject of Jesus' ancestry. They were concerned both with internal attacks of heretical Christian groups such as the Gnostics, as well as external attacks from opposing Jewish religious leaders. Early Christian tradition, doubtlessly reinforced by the eloquent tongue and descriptive pen of St. Paul, unhesitatingly identified Jesus as a descendant of King David, the most royal blood in Israel. It was a fulfillment of Isaiah's prophecy that:

> And there shall come forth a rod out of the stem of Jesse, and a Branch shall grow out of his roots.
>
> (Isaiah 11:1)

The second-century philosopher, Justin Martyr, persuasively argued that by the will of God Jesus was conceived by the Virgin Mary who was, according to him, a lineal descendant of Jacob and Judah. Similarly, St. Ignatius of Antioch (d.c. A.D. 107) was the first early church writer to emphasize the virgin birth of Jesus, advancing the idea that Jesus was at once both human and divine, from Mary and from God. Early Christian theologians, Irenaeus and Tertullian, responding to Gnostic ideas regarding the humanity of Jesus, declared Jesus to be not only a descendant of the house of David through Mary's lineage, but also a son of God through the virgin birth.

For one thousand years in both the Eastern and Western churches, the Mosaic law of Levirate marriage dominated an understanding of Jesus' roots. Advanced by the pens of Julius Africanus and Eusebius of Caesarea in the third and fourth centuries, the theme was carried forward in the theological writings of St. Jerome and St. Augustine. The theological writings of Albertus Magnus and Thomas Aquinas in the thirteenth century restate and echo not only Julius Africanus' position on Jesus' genealogy but what had also become the traditional position of writers.

The Continental Church reformers, Ulrich Zwingli, John Calvin and Martin Luther wrote little about Jesus' roots. Their minds and pens were taken up with a variety of other key theological doctrines as well as Church practices. Further refinement or restatement of Jesus' roots was to await the declaration of the Doctrine of Immaculate Conception by Pope Pius IX on December 8, 1854.

German, French and English scholars of the late nineteenth and early twentieth centuries hoped to recover and write a biography of Jesus on the basis of the Gospels as the earliest documents on the life of Jesus. The task proved to be difficult, if not impossible. Reconstructing the life of Jesus and the early church during the period of the apostles was a project too modern, too complex and too ambitious. It was an error to consider the few Gospels and the rest of the New Testament in such a way. For what we have, instead of a full-blown life of Jesus, are the four Gospel accounts which are to be read and studied with patience, care and inspiration for an understanding of "who" Jesus was. The challenge for the reader and listener today remains the same as it was in the first century. After twenty centuries, there are no shortcuts to our understanding of Jesus; it is primarily a religious task, and not a secular one.

There are very few references to Jesus outside of the New Testament books. He is almost unheard of in Jewish or Roman literature of his time. However, the distinguished Roman historian of the second century, Tacitus, recorded Jesus' execution by order of Pontius Pilate during the reign of Tiberius (*Annals* 15:44), and the first-century Jewish historian, Flavius Josephus, wrote a book on the history of Judaism which mentioned:

> Now there was about this time Jesus, a wise man, if it be lawful to call him a man, for he was a doer of wonderful works, a teacher of such men as receive the truth with pleasure. He drew over to him both many of the Jews and many of the Gentiles. He was [the] Christ. And when Pilate, at the suggestion of the principal men among us, had condemned him to the cross, those that

loved him at the first did not forsake him; for he appeared to
them alive again the third day; as the divine things concerning
him. And the tribe of Christians so named from him are not ex-
tinct to this day.

> *Antiquities of*
> *the Jews,* Bk. XVII, Ch. III
> Sec. 3)

The Roman writer Lucian rejected Christians and portrayed
Jesus as "the man who was crucified in Palestine because he introduced this new cult into the world" (*The Passing of Pere-
grinus,* pp. 13, 15).

These remarks came from the pens of men who were not
friendly to Jesus and Christianity, and not informed about it. Yet
their comments are valuable as they substantiate the fact that
Jesus did indeed live, that he enjoyed a popular audience, and
that Christianity was widespread by the early decades of the second century.

The task of reconsidering and writing on the subject of Jesus'
roots inevitably leads one beyond the rigorous boundaries of historical training. There are indeed aspects of his genealogy for
which we will never have a thorough and complete answer. But
that does not mean the topic is forever closed to review and discussion. We know that Jesus lived and that he lived in one of the
smallest, most insignificant and distant provinces of the far-
stretched Roman Empire. We know, too, that he was not an author, that he did not write books—or if he did the pages have not
survived. He had little impact on the affairs of his time beyond
his own circle of disciples. Yet he changed the course of world
history as no man ever has. While his name is known today
throughout the world and he is worshipped as the Son of God by
a large portion of the world's population, during his lifetime he
was essentially unknown outside his own province of Judaea.

One of the primary purposes of the study of genealogy is to
answer the question: "From whence have we come?" What are
the names of our eight great-grandparents? Where did they live,
and what kind of work did they do? These are universal interests
on the part of men and women everywhere about themselves
and their own families. The same principles and questions have

been asked with no less enthusiasm of Jesus' roots. We want to know from whence he came because his impact on the world has been so strong and permanent. His impact was spiritual, as both the Son of Man and Son of God. He was the image of God on earth, dressed in humanity and divinity.

The roots of Jesus lie at the roots of our own being and purpose. The questions, Who are we? Where did we come from? Where are we going? are at once simple and complex. The continuing search down the ages for Jesus' ancestry is indeed a search for our own physical and spiritual ancestors. While we may content ourselves with the momentary and fleeting security of concrete evidence and facts and empirical analysis which are the domain of the historians and scientists, they are not enough. Ultimately we are creatures who seek meaning and purpose in our lives. It is this quest which leads us along the path of religion, faith and intuition. It is a path which has its own method of knowing.

Jesus' appeal is at once both charismatic and intellectual. The forcefulness of his moral teaching has had no equal, and the power of his ministry remains unmatched. He has been a master model for all men and women.

GLOSSARY

AMMONITES

The name of the Semitic descendants of Benammi, Lot's younger son by his daughter, and who was born in a cave near Zoar. They were regarded as relatives of the Israelites, who were charged to treat them kindly. The Ammonites flourished as a separate political state on the edges of the Syrian Desert, east of the Dead Sea, in central Transjordan between about 1300 and 480 B.C. Their capital was Rabbathammon, the present Ammon, Jordan.

The Ammonites became long-standing enemies of Israel and an element for spiritual corruption. They were not only cheered by the misfortunes which overtook the devoted of Israel, but delighted in spreading their false gods and undermining ideals through intermarriage.

ARAMEANS

A semitic people who were traditionally considered as descendants of Shem or of the family of Nahor. The exact origin of the Arameans is not known, but they seemed to have formed part of the mass migration of nomads that moved northward through the western edges of the Syrian Desert from Egypt, past Canaan to the lands along the Euphrates River. As early as about 3100 B.C., the Arameans had appeared in Egypt.

In the Old Testament, the Arameans were identified with the Syrians, at times warring with Israel, and at other times being acknowledged as relatives. It was among the Arameans that Abraham sent to obtain a wife for his son, Isaac. Still later, David's attack on their powerful fortress, Zobah, helped save Assyria from attack by the Arameans. During the ninth and eighth centuries B.C., the Arameans were a key enemy of Israel.

ARIANISM

A Christian heresy founded in the fourth century by Arius (c. A.D. 256–336), a priest in Alexandria. According to Arius' teachings, God created, before all things, a Son who was the first being, but who was neither equal nor eternal with the Father. It was Arius' position that Jesus was a supernatural being, not really human and not really divine, but more like a half-god. In these opinions Arius followed the ideas of Lucian, who was a disciple of the heretic Paul of Samosata.

Condemned and deprived of his office in A.D. 321, Arius went to Asia and advanced his doctrines among the people through popular sermons and songs. With the aid of powerful leaders Arius' doctrines were declared orthodox in Asia Minor. As civil as well as religious peace was disturbed, Constantine summoned the first Ecumenical Council at Nicaea. Arius' theological position was anathematized by the Council of Nicaea and banished by Constantine in A.D. 325. Nonetheless, the issues continued to divide the church, East and West, as well as the imperial leaders for the next half century.

Arianism was outlawed in A.D. 379 when the Catholic Theolosius I became emperor of the East. The first Council of Constantinople in A.D. 318 reaffirmed the Nicaean statements, and Arianism within the Roman Empire seems shortly thereafter to have disappeared.

ASSYRIANS

The country of these ancient peoples lay in the upper Mesopotamian plain, bounded on the west by the Syrian desert, on the south by the Jebel Hamrin and Babylonia, and on the north and east by the Urartian and Persian hills. The most densely populated and fertile area of Assyria lay east of the Tigris River. The ancient empire of Assyria developed about 2300 B.C. around the city of Ashur on the upper Tigris and south of what was later to become its capital city, Nineveh.

The Assyrians were dreaded by both Israel and Judah. The Assyrian armies were interpreted by the biblical prophets to be inflictions of God to punish the waywardness of his chosen people. The Assyrians achieved their greatest power during the reign of Ashurbanipal (c. 669–c. 633 B.C.), with their empire extending southward into northern Arabia and as far away as Thebes in Egypt, westward into Cappadocia, northward to Lake Van and Lake Urmiah, and eastward into Elam.

CANAANITES

The land of the Canaanites was the same territory as ancient Palestine, lying between the Jordan River, Dead Sea and the Mediterranean. To the east of Canaan were the kingdoms of Moab and Sihon, and to the south, Edom. The Canaanites were one of several groups of Semites occupying this territory at the time of Israel's invasions during the fourteenth through twelfth centuries B.C. Gradually, the Canaanites were pushed seaward, and by the early twelfth century B.C., they held only the coastal strip of North Palestine and South Syria, an area called Phoenicia.

The Canaanites contributed significantly to the culture of the Hebrews. Their language was the basis for Hebrew Scripture, and their influence was strong in Hebrew music and musical instruments, ceramic arts and architecture. Canaanite cities, such as Jericho, Lachish and Megiddo, were well-built fortifications of temples and palaces, superior both in style and craftmanship to similar Hebrew sites.

COVENANT

In the Bible and in theology the covenant is the agreement or engagement of God with man as revealed in the Scriptures. Sometimes it was an agreement between God and an individual, such as God and Noah or God and Abraham; and at other times a covenant could also be fashioned between individuals, such as Abraham and Abimelech or Jonathan and David.

The idea of the covenant between the God of Israel and his people is central to the religion of the Old Testament. It is the pledge that Yahweh will be the God and Israel his people.

CYRUS THE GREAT

Founder of the Persian Empire, he was the son of Cambyses I, King of Anshan, and of Mandane, daughter of King Astyages of the Medes. He succeeded to the throne of Anshan about 559 B.C. and immediately set out to conquer surrounding territories. Ultimately, Cyrus became ruler of the largest empire the world had yet seen, the Persian Empire.

By 550 B.C., Cyrus had united his own people and conquered the Medes; by 547 B.C., he had vanquished Lydia; and in 539 B.C., he had defeated the Chaldean army at Babylon. When his son, Cambyses II, succeeded him in 530 B.C., he took Egypt, and the Achaemenid house controlled the entire territory east as far as India.

Cyrus figures prominently in the Bible, where he is viewed by Isaiah as God's appointed agent, and was also given approval by Daniel. He was known for his leniency to all captured peoples, and allowed the Jews to return from their captivity in Babylon to Jerusalem and rebuild the Jerusalem Temple.

DARIUS THE GREAT

As king of ancient Persia (522–486 B.C.), the early years of Darius' reign were spent in suppressing revolts in Persia, Media, Babylonia and the East. He proved himself to be a worthy successor of Cyrus the Great, both in military prowess and imperial administrative skill. He launched a campaign against the Greeks which resulted in his defeat at the memorable battle of Marathon in 490 B.C. However, he consolidated Persian power in the East, including northwest India. Darius continued Cyrus' policy of restoring the Jewish state, and under his direction the rebuilding of the Temple in Jerusalem was completed in 515 B.C. It is for this reason he is mentioned favorably in Ezra, Haggai and Zechariah.

THE DEAD SEA SCROLLS

One of the greatest discoveries of biblical archeology was the find in 1947, and in subsequent years, in caves above the northwestern corner of the Dead Sea of fragmentary remains of what had once been a large library. The most important of these so-called Dead Sea Scrolls are the Qumram texts. Archeologists believe that the neighborhood was the headquarters for a Jewish community, probably a branch of the Essenes. A cemetery and a complex of buildings have been uncovered at the site of the Qumram community, as well as the scrolls, which were found in jars. All of these finds indicate that the community flourished between the first century B.C. and the first half of the first century A.D.

The documents which have been found in the caves have been of significant value to historians, archeologists and paleographers, providing a new understanding of the text of the Old Testament and of the people of Qumram and their influence on the early Christian movement. Before the discovery of the Dead Sea Scrolls, the oldest nearly complete manuscripts of the Hebrew Old Testament were from about the tenth century A.D. or almost a thousand years later. Dramatic parallels in thought and expression between the Qumram texts and the New Testament, particularly the Gospel according to John, have led to wide speculation with regard to the Essene influence on Christianity. Some scholars have even suggested, for example, that Jesus and John the Baptist were members of this Essene sect.

DOCETISM

An early heretical position in Christian thought which claimed that Jesus was a mere phantasm who only seemed to live and suffer.

Docetists believed that Jesus had not come in the flesh, that rather he only seemed to have a physical body. Docetism presumed a dualistic view of the world wherein it would have been impossible for a divine being to assume human flesh, and while Docetists did not doubt Jesus' divinity, they did question and deny his humanity. Docetism was generally similar to most Gnostic systems.

EBIONITES

A Jewish-Christian sect of rural Palestine during the first centuries after Jesus. According to the theologian Origen, they were of two groups. The Judaic Ebionites observed closely the Mosaic law and regarded Jesus as a miracle-working prophet and St. Paul as a renegade. Gnostic Ebionites believed Jesus to be a Spirit, invisible to men, and gave to him the title Prophet of the Truth.

EDOMITES

Descendants of Esau, who possibly came from Aram originally, the Edomites occupied a territory that extended along the eastern border of the Arabah valley from the Dead Sea to Elath on the Gulf of Aqaba. Their history is one of continuous conflict and warfare with their Jewish, Assyrian and Syrian neighbors. They were finally conquered by the Maccabees in 164 B.C. and subsequently merged in with the Jews.

The biblical stories in Genesis, as well as references in the prophetic books, emphasize the close racial ties between Israelites and Edomites.

ESSENES

The Essenes were an important Jewish religious community which flourished during the first century B.C. and first century A.D. It was one of the three Jewish schools of thought in the ancient period; the others being the Sadducees and Pharisees. Key sources regarding the teachings and practices of the Essenes are the writings of the historian Josephus and the philosopher Philo of Alexandria. Philo estimated the number of Essenes at about four thousand, living primarily in villages and working hard as farmers. They devoted much time to the communal study of moral and religious questions, as well as studying the scriptures.

We are nearly certain that one of the Essene communities was located at Qumram and brought to our attention with the discovery in 1947 of The Dead Sea Scrolls.

GNOSTICISM

Gnosticism was a dualistic philosophic and religious movement of the late Hellenistic and early Christian periods. The word signifies a wide variety of sects existing during the second century A.D. and promising salvation through a "knowledge" that they claimed was revealed to them alone. The origins of Gnosticism are traced to the Jewish Cabbals, Hellenistic mystery cults and Babylonian and Egyptian mythology. Much of early Christian doctrine was formulated in response to the ideas of such Gnostic writers as Valentinus and Basilides. Their writings were viewed as a serious threat to the church.

Gnosticism taught that the world is ruled by evil archons, among them the deity of the Old Testament, who hold captive the spirit of man. Jesus is identified as an aeon sent from the spiritual universe to restore the long-lost knowledge of man's divine origin. Gnostics held secret principles which they believed would free them at death from the evil archons and restore them to their heavenly abode.

Our knowledge of the Gnostic sects comes from two sources. First, the writings of the early church fathers, particularly in Irenaeus' work *Against Heresies*. Second, from the Gnostic writings found in 1945 near Nag Hammadi in upper Egypt.

HERMETISM

A philosophical school of thought addressing, primarily, the idea of the complete community of all beings and objects. A collection of writings associated with the name of "Hermes Trismegistos" ("Thrice-great Hermes") were attributed to the Egyptian god of wisdom, Thoth. The books treat many different subjects including magic, astrology and alchemy and were particularly influential in the third century with the Neoplatonist thinkers.

HEROD THE GREAT

A son of the second Antipater (fl. c. 65 B.C.) of the dynasty which ruled Palestine during the time of Jesus. He ruled as Procurator of Judaea between 37 and 4 B.C. Bold, brilliant and enterprising, his power was fashioned as a friend and ally of Rome. He advanced the Roman emperor's cultural policy with opulent building projects. In Jerusalem, he built for himself a palace on the west wall, although the greatest of all his building enterprises was the reconstruction of the Jerusalem Temple begun early in 19 B.C.

Herod was not esteemed by the Jewish people despite his lavish efforts to rebuild the Temple. His Edomite ancestry was not forgotten, and his extermination of the Hasmonean family could not be forgiven. His suspicious nature is illustrated by the story of the Magi and the slaughter of the infants of Bethlehem. Indeed, Herod is probably best remembered for his murderous outbursts, which edged on insanity, than for his extraordinary administrative ability.

KOINE GREEK

The non-literary Hellenistic Greek is generally called the *Koine*. This Greek word usually describes the terms "language" or "dialect" and means the "common language." It was the language of the common people who were unschooled. There was no standard form of *Koine*, its use varying from individual to individual. *Koine* was the common language of the Mediterranean world in the sense that it was not a dialect, restricted to a specific geographical area. Rather it was a vigorous, lively language open to the use of daily living. A major source for the study of *Koine* is the Greek Bible. The New Testament portion was originally written in Greek, while the Old Testament is a translation.

MACCABEES

The Maccabees were a Jewish family of the second and first century B.C. who led an epic struggle for the restoration of Jewish political and religious life against Hellenistic culture and imperialism. According to the historian Josephus, the family name seems to have been Hasmon, thus they are called Hasmoneans or Asmoneans in the rabbinic literature.

It was Judas Maccabeus who led the fight for religious freedom against the Seleucid King Antiochus IV (Epiphanes) of Syria (175–163 B.C.). The Maccabean uprising followed the efforts by Antiochus IV to impose Hellenistic culture on the Jews and to destroy Judaism itself. Antiochus had taken advantage of divisions among the Jews and had stripped and desecrated the Temple.

A leader in the manner of Gideon, Judas Maccabeus employed guerilla warfare, and his forces defeated the Syrian forces sent against them. Triumphantly entering Jerusalem, he purified the Temple, where for three years sacrifices had been made to Zeus, and reestablished the worship of Yahweh. Hannukkah, or the Feast of the Dedi-

cation, or "Feast of the Maccabees," was instituted to honor the re-
dedication of the Temple.

Judas was killed in battle in 161 B.C., and succeeded in turn by his
brothers Jonathan and Simon who continued the fight against Syria.
In 142 B.C. Simon succeeded in negotiating a treaty with Demetrius
II, the Seleucid king, by which the Jews achieved political independence, and thereby establishing the Maccabean or Hasmonean dynasty.

MOABITES

The Moabites were the descendants of Moab, son of Lot by his in-
cestuous union with his eldest daughter. The land of Moab lay amid
the fertile plateau of the Jordan River, East of the Dead Sea. It was
directly across from Bethlehem, birthplace of David and Jesus, both
of whom had Moabite blood through their descent from Ruth the
Moabitess.

In language and background the Moabite people had much in common with Israel. The relations between Moab and Judah are frequently mentioned in the Bible; however, Moabite spiritual practices
did not approach the elevated heights of pure Hebrew worship. Hebrew prophets frequently condemned Moab's inferior level of religious worship.

Moab came to an end as a political entity after the invasion of
Tiglath-pileser III about 733 B.C. Its people were then absorbed by
the Nabataeans during the second and first centuries B.C. and the first
century A.D.

PATRIARCHS

In the biblical tradition a patriarch is denoted in several ways: as
the male head of a long family line; as one of the founders of the
human race before the Flood, such as the lists in Genesis descending
from Cain and Seth to Lamech; and finally as one of the early fathers
from the time of the Flood to the birth of Abraham. Still later, the
term patriarch is used to identify one of the ancestors of the Jews,
such as Abraham, Isaac and Jacob and sometimes the twelve sons of
Jacob from whom the tribes of Israel are descended. According to
scholars today, these Patriarchs of the Old Testament lived from the
twenty-first to nineteenth centuries B.C. They were leaders of a nomadic people who wandered the hills of central and southern
Palestine, ranging as far south as the Negeb. For the Hebrew Patriarchs, Yahweh, their God, was near and real to them. The Patriarch

was recognized by his people as "a friend of God," who was told things by God.

PHARISEES

The Pharisees were one of the three important philosophical sects of Judaism during the two centuries just before and just after the birth of Jesus. The work of the Pharisees began after the dynasty of the Maccabees succeeded in delivering their people from Syria's grip, and during a time when John Hyrcanus, who was high priest (135–105 B.C.), had established a secular principate.

The Pharisees insisted upon a strict observance of the Law as applied to all of life. Beside the Torah the Pharisees placed great importance on the Oral Law which upheld and advanced the customs and practices that had become popular. Emphasis was placed on annotation of the Scriptures so that they might be used by the people. As all of life fell more closely under the regulations of religious observance, doctrines and rules were clarified and increased.

The Pharisees believed in baptism, free will, life after death, the coming of the Messiah and the Day of Judgment. By the age of Jesus, however, many of the common people had become estranged from the Pharisees. However, after the fall of the Temple and the destruction of Jerusalem in A.D. 70, the synagogues and schools of the Pharisees alone continued to operate and promote Judaism. Active until about A.D. 135, Pharisasism continued to the subsequent development of orthodox Judaism.

PHILISTINES

A non-Semitic sea people who came to Palestine from the Aegean region, probably Crete, in the twelfth century B.C. They occupied a coastal strip of territory about fifty miles long and fifteen miles wide that extended along the Mediterranean from Joppa to the south of Gaza. The Philistines became one of the Israelites' chief rivals for centuries. Their control of iron supplies and their effective political organization based on an association of great cities, allowed the tiny country of Philistia to remain a threat to Israel until the time of King David's victories over them.

A collision course was inevitable between the strong and ambitious Philistines and the Israelites. Both peoples arrived in Canaan about the same time although the Philistines affiliated themselves with the Canaanites, adopting some of the Canaanite language and gods. Situated along the Mediterranean coast, the Philistines were exposed to attacks from Egypt and Assyria in the last third of the eighth century and throughout the seventh century B.C. After an extraordinary siege, Alexander the Great captured the city of Gaza in 332 B.C., and subsequently the Philistines were absorbed by other neighboring peoples.

PROPHETS

The prophets were the religious leaders of Israel, particularly during the period of the kingdoms and the Babylonian captivity. The major prophets are: Isaiah, Jeremiah, Ezekiel and Daniel. The minor prophets are: Hosea, Joel, Amos, Obadiah, Jonah, Micah, Nahum, Habakkuk, Zephaniah, Haggai, Zechariah and Malachi.

The prophet was believed to be inspired by God to guide the chosen people. Some prophets, convinced of their divine mission to cleanse Israel's religion, attacked the whole fabric of life, coming to the forefront as advocates for the poor and oppressed and as leaders in social reform. Their message was that Israel could be reconciled with God only by complete purification in religion and in state. The books of the various prophets are some of the most attractive passages in the Old Testament.

SADDUCEES

The Sadducees were not a sect, school of philosophy or a political party. Rather, they were a priestly, aristocratic faction. Active during the first century B.C. and first century A.D., their interest focused on the Temple and they were in strong opposition to the views and practices of the Pharisees. The Sadducees accepted only the Hebrew Scriptures and not the oral tradition held by the Pharisees. They did not believe in immortality, resurrection, the existence of demons and angels or the coming of the Messiah. The Sadducees represented the wealthy, established interests of the Jews in Jerusalem. After the revolt against Rome in A.D. 70 and the destruction of the Temple, they were no longer influential.

SELEUCIDS

The Seleucids were a dynasty of rulers who ruled over Bactria, Persia, Babylonia, Syria and part of Asia Minor between 312 and 64 B.C. The founder of the family was Seleucus I, Nicator, who as a young man accompanied Alexander the Great (356–323 B.C.) during his Asiatic and India campaigns. Antioch was the capital of the turbulent and tyrannical Seleucid Empire.

Palestine came under Seleucid rule in 198 B.C., when Antiochus III defeated Egypt in a battle near the Jordan headwaters. The Seleucids ruled from 175 B.C. until 63 B.C. when Rome conquered Palestine. The Seleucid dynasty ended with Pompey's reduction of Syria to a mere Roman province in 64 B.C.

STOICS

The Stoics were a school of Greek philosophy founded by Zeno about the beginning of the third century B.C. They were called "Stoics" because they met in the Stoac Poecile, or painted porch, at Athens, to hear their teacher, Zeno, lecture. This school of philosophy was particularly strong during the New Testament period of the Roman Empire. Seneca, Epicletus and Marcus Aurelius were great Stoic teachers.

The aim of the Stoics was to shape men's characters to meet the difficulties of this world, and their doctrines were also shaped toward this end. The ethics of Stoicism stated that a man's soul is part of the divine soul and that a life of virtue is in conformity with nature. Therefore, the highest goal of human life is virtue, which men can achieve only by bringing their wills into conformity with the laws of nature.

The Apostle Paul met Stoic philosophers at Athens and was ridiculed by them as a "babbler" and a promoter of "strange gods" because he preached about Jesus and the Resurrection. Nevertheless, many Stoic teachings parallel those of Christianity.

SYNOPTIC GOSPELS

The first three Gospels, Matthew, Mark and Luke, are considered as a unit and referred to by scholars as the Synoptic Gospels. They have greater similarity to one another than any one of them has to the Gospel of John.

ZEALOT

The Jewish historian Josephus identified a Zealot as a member of a fourth group of Jews, distinguished from the Pharisees, Sadducees and Essenes. Zealots were strict interpreters of the Mosaic law and were probably founded by Judas the Galilean who led a revolt in A.D. 6 against Rome. The Zealots opposed the payment of a tax by Israel to a pagan emperor as treason toward God, Israel's true king. Although the revolt of A.D. 6 was crushed, the Zealot movement remained alive and surfaced actively during the war against Rome between A.D. 66 and 73. The last Zealot stronghold, Masada, fell in May, A.D. 74.

BIBLIOGRAPHY

SUGGESTIONS FOR FURTHER READING

The following list of books is a selected bibliography designed with the interests and needs of the general reader in mind. They are all written in English by scholars distinguished in their fields. While that qualification is ever important, I have also been guided by the author's engaging and informed literary style. Most scholars seem to write only for themselves or a small circle of colleagues rather than for a broader more popular audience. As some lecturers, droning on at the lecture desk, are able to easily put us to sleep, so too are many scholarly books. Accordingly, I commend to you for your further reading the following books, all of which will guide and entertain the reader in a graceful manner.

Ashe, Geoffrey, *The Virgin* (London: Paladin, 1977).

Barrow, R.H., *The Romans* (New York: Penguin, 1949).

Barthell, Edward E., Jr., *Gods and Goddesses of Ancient Greece* (Coral Gables, Fla.: University of Miami Press, 1971).

Brown, Raymond, E., S.G., *The Birth of the Messiah. A Commentary on the Infancy Narratives in Matthew and Luke* (New York: Image Books, Doubleday, 1979).

Brown, R.E., Donfried, K.P., Fitzmyer, J.A., and Reumann, J., Eds. *Mary in the New Testament* (Philadelphia: Fortress Press, 1978).

Campbell, Joseph, *The Masks of God: Occidental Mythology* (New York: Penguin, 1976).

Chadwick, Henry, *The Early Church* (New York: Penguin, 1967).

Chadwick, Owen, *The Reformation* (New York: Penguin, 1972).

Crawford, Michael, *The Roman Republic* (London: Fontana, 1978).

Cream, C.W., *Gods, Graves and Scholars: The Story of Archaeology* (New York: Bantam, 1967).

Davies, A. Powell, *The Meaning of the Dead Sea Scrolls* (New York: New American Library, 1956).

Dimont, Max I., *Jews, God and History* (New York: New American Library, 1962).

Early Christian Writings: The Apostolic Fathers. Translated by Maxwell Staniforth (New York: Penguin, 1968).

Finely, M.I., *Aspects of Antiquity, Discoveries and Controversies* (New York: Penguin, 1977). Second edition.

——, *The Ancient Greeks* (New York; Penguin, 1963).

——, *The World of Odysseus* (New York: Penguin, 1979). Second edition.

Grant, Michael, *Jesus, an Historian's Review of the Gospels* (New York: Scribner's, 1977).

——, *Myths of the Greeks and Romans* (New York: New American Library, 1962).

Graves, Robert, *King Jesus* (New York: Farrar, Straus, Giroux, 1946).

——, *The Greek Myths* (New York: Penguin, 1960), 2 volumes.

Grayzel, Solomon, *A History of the Jews, From the Babylonian Exile to the Present,* 5728–1968 (New York: New American Library, 1968).

Hamilton, Edith, *Mythology* (New York: New American Library, 1942).

Jaeger, Werner, *Early Christianity and Greek Paideia* (Cambridge: Harvard University Press, 1961).

Josephus, *The Jewish War* (New York: Penguin, 1980).

Keller, Werner, *The Bible as History. A Confirmation of the Book of Books* (New York: Bantam, 1974).

Kramer, Samuel Noah, Ed., *Mythologies of the New Testament* (New York: Anchor Books, Doubleday, 1961).

Murray, Oswyn, *Early Greece* (London: Fontana, 1980).

Pagels, Elaine, *The Gnostic Gospels* (New York: Random House, 1979).

Pettinato, Giovanni, *The Archives of Ebla. An Empire Inscribed in Clay* (New York: Doubleday, 1981).

Potok, Chaim, *Wonderings, Chaim Potok's History of the Jews* (New York: Fawcett Crest, 1978).

Russell, Bertrand, *A History of Western Philosophy* (New York: Simon & Schuster, 1945).

Southern, R.W., *Western Society and the Church in the Middle Ages* (New York: Penguin, 1970).

Velikovsky, Immanuel, *Ramses II and His Time* (London: Abacus, 1978).

Vermes, Geza, *The Dead Sea Scrolls in English* (New York: Penguin, 1975). Second edition.

Vidler, Alec R., *The Church in an Age of Revolution, 1789 to the Present Day* (New York: Penguin, 1971).

Walbank, F.W., *The Hellenistic World* (London: Fontana, 1981).

White, J.E.M., *Ancient Egypt: Its Culture and History* (New York: Dover, 1970).

ATLASES

Frank, Harry Thomas, *Discovering the Biblical World* (Maplewood, N.J.: Hammond, 1975).

Grollenberg, Luc. H., *The Penguin Shorter Atlas of the Bible* (New York: Penguin, 1978).

May, Herbert G., Ed., *Oxford Bible Atlas* (London: Oxford University Press, 1968).

INDEX

JAMES B. BELL serves as Director of the New-York Historical Society, one of the leading institutions of its kind in the world. He holds a B.A. from the University of Minnesota, a Masters Degree in Divinity from the Episcopal Theological School in Cambridge, Massachusetts, and a D. Phil. degree from Balliol College, Oxford University. He has taught at Princeton University and Ohio State University. He took over from Gilbert H. Doane and upon the latter's death became the principal author of *Searching for Your Ancestors*, the classic book on tracing genealogies.

LOCATIONS AND DATES OF EARLY CHRISTIAN WRITERS